D0736096

The Relational Disciple

How God Uses Community to Shape Followers of Jesus

Joel Comiskey

Published By CCS Publishing

 CCS Publishing

www.joelcomiskeygroup.com

Copyright © 2010 by Joel Comiskey

Published by CCS Publishing
23890 Brittlebush Circle
Moreno Valley, CA 92557 USA
1-888-344-CELL

All rights reserved. No part of this publication may be reproduced, stored in a retrieval system, or transmitted, in any form or by any means, electronic, mechanical, photocopying, recording, or otherwise, without the prior written permission of the publisher.
Printed in the United States of America.

Cover design by Josh Talbot
Editing by Scott Boren
Copy editing by Brian McClemore and Susan Osborn

All Scripture quotations, unless otherwise indicated, are from the Holy Bible, New International Version, Copyright ©1973, 1978, 1984 by International Bible Society. Used by permission.

CCS Publishing is the book-publishing division of Joel Comiskey Group, a resource and coaching ministry dedicated to equipping leaders for cell-based ministry.
Find us on the World Wide Web at **www.joelcomiskeygroup.com**

Publisher's Cataloging-in-Publication
  (Provided by Quality Books, Inc.)
Comiskey, Joel, 1956-
      The relational disciple : how God uses community to
  shape followers of Jesus / Joel Comiskey.
      p. cm.
      Includes bibliographical references and index.
      LCCN 2009900120
      ISBN-13: 978-0-9790679-9-0
      ISBN-10: 0-9790679-9-5
      1. Fellowship--Religious aspects--Christianity.
  2. Interpersonal relations--Religious aspects--
  Christianity. 3. Spiritual formation. I. Title.
  BV4517.5.C66 2009   248.4
                    QBI09-600178

Praise for *The Relational Disciple*

"Joel Comiskey has not only shown us the need for relational disciples in our culture of isolationism, but he's also instructed us on how to become relational disciples. You'll discover how to practice the one-anothers of Scripture in daily life, how to be successful with those closest to you, and how small group community will transform you and those without Christ. I enthusiastically recommend this book."

— **RANDY FRAZEE** Senior Minister of Oak Hills Church, author of bestselling books on community

"*The Relational Disciple* underscores the radical truth that Christian formation happens primarily in the context of relational community. Life-shaping occurs when we come to "know" and allow ourselves to be "known." Chat rooms, texting, and even e-mails permit us to communicate in selective anonymity today. As Southwest Airlines reminds: "You can't fax a handshake, mail a hug, or have a family reunion by e-mail." While impression can take place at a distance—impact only occurs in some degree of closeness. This book will challenge today's widespread acculturated western individualism. The identity of a true disciple of Jesus Christ is not created in isolation or at a distance. Experiencing life in Jesus is wrapped in "familiness" to allow us to thrive. That means we learn to be loved and accepted—to belong! So read and understand how to become what God has created us to be as brothers and sisters who in our togetherness reflect the Son, the Father, and the Spirit of Jesus in His world today."

— **JULIE GORMAN** Professor of Christian Formation and Discipleship, Fuller Theological Seminary, Pasadena, California

"*The Relational Disciple* is an excellent help for believers, group leaders and pastoral staff alike. I especially appreciated Joel's transparency, as he shared appropriate and insightful bits of his personal journey. Dr. Comiskey makes a case for "not forsaking the assembly of yourselves together" persuasively and inspirationally. His writing style is fresh, illustrations joyful, and arguments powerful. And all this in a book that is brief enough to encourage reading by non-readers! I want to recommend it to every church leader who has hoped for a way to promote effective evangelism in her or his church. It is so true that belonging precedes believing. By following Comiskey's teaching, whole churches -- *large or small* -- could be transformed into more hospitable places where soul comfort and growth are stimulated. Thank you, Dr. Comiskey for writing this book."

— **CARL GEORGE** Consultant and author of many books, including, *Nine Keys to Effective Small Group Leadership.*

Praise for *The Relational Disciple*

"If one wants to catch a glimpse of the core changes needed for the church of the 21st Century, this is a crucial book. Joel Comiskey integrates good biblical theology and Christ-centered practice, with sensitivity to historical theology and western cultural resistance. This is a practical and accessible book for all who desire to reorient the church to an ancient and future pattern of relational disciple-making. The Contemporary Church is called to repent of inadequate ministry models, and be transformed by the full nature, being, and activity of God in Jesus Christ, by the power of the Holy Spirit in the reality of everyday human life. It is a brief but important read for every church leader."
— **THE REV. DR. GARETH ICENOGLE** Senior Pastor, Westside Presbyterian Church, Ridgewood, New Jersey

"Joel has done a brilliant job of explaining the way back from the consumer-driven individualism and isolationism found in the American church today. Each chapter provides wonderful ideas for small groups and individuals who want to be highly relational disciples of Christ."
— **RANDALL NEIGHBOUR** Author of *The Naked Truth about Small Group Ministry* and President of TOUCH Outreach Ministries, Houston, Texas

"*The Relational Disciple* is a significant book for today. It explicitly deals with the individualism that has crept into society at large as well as into the Church and describes and gives value to the importance of relationships and how we are discipled and changed through a relational process. It goes on to describe how this relational process is also how we do mission in the context of a wider world. I believe this book is really important. Through the credit crunch that is affecting us all we have seen the downside of individualism and people doing things without realizing their relational context or impact. This book will inspire us to be a part of community and to build community and to be changed in this process."

— **LAURENCE SINGLEHURST** Director of Cell UK , worldwide speaker, and author of several books

Table of Contents

Table of Contents   5
Acknowledgements   9
Introduction   11
   Anonymity in the Church   11
   The Way of the Master   13
   My Own Journey   14
Section I: Seeing Discipleship from a Different
Perspective   19
Chapter 1: Conformed to the Pattern of Individualism   21
   The Western World's Culture of individualism   22
   Individualism and Others   25
   On the Move   27
   Media Isolation   28
   The Church Mirrors Society   30
   Getting Back to Relational Discipleship   32
Chapter 2: Transformed by the Trinity   35
   What Is the Trinity?   37
   The Trinity and Community   39
   The Trinity Working in Us   42
Chapter 3: Transformed by One Another   45
   Focusing on Others   46
   Love one Another   47
   Serve one Another   48
   Forgive Each Other   49
   Build Up Each Other   51
   Encourage Each Other   52
   Be Kind to One Another   53
   Be Devoted to One Another   54

Table of Contents

Accountability 55
Instruct One Another 55
Submit to One Another 57
Confess Sins to One Another 58
Interdependence 60
Walk in Humility with One Another 60
Accept One Another 61
Live at Peace with One Another 63
Bear with Each Other 64
Wait for One Another 65
Honor One Another 66
Use Your Gift among Each Other 67
Show Hospitality to One Another 68
Watchfulness 69
Do Not Lie to Each Other 69
Do Not Fight with Each Other 71
Do Not Envy One Another 72
Do Not Judge One Another 73
God's Empowerment 74
Chapter 4: Transformed by Conflict 75
Do Not Run 76
Care Enough to Confront 78
Forgive Those Who Offend You 80
Rebuild Trust 85
Forgiving and Forgiven 87
Section II: Practicing Relational Discipleship 89
Chapter 5: Practicing Relational Discipleship with the Inner Circle 91
Those Closest to You 93
Priorities 94
Spouse 95
Family 98
Spiritual Growth 99

Table of Contents

Be Real 100
A Secure Environment 101
Friends 102
Chapter 6: Practicing Relational Discipleship in an Organic Circle 107
Small Enough to Care 109
What Happens in a Micro Church 111
Freedom to Share 113
Learning from the Methodists 115
Everyone Needs a Family 118
Connecting Micro with Macro 119
Accountability 121
Chapter 7: Practicing Relational Discipleship in a Mission Circle 125
Learning from Saint Patrick 126
Evangelism as a Group Event 130
Transparent Sharing 132
Developing Relationships 133
God is Transforming Us 137
Appendix 1: Training for Relational Disciples 139
Appendix 2: Resources by Joel Comiskey 143
Index 151
Endnotes 157

Acknowledgements

Although I'm the author of this book, I've had plenty of help along the way. In the long process to make this book a reality, many hands and eyes have handled and contributed to the final work. Several people deserve special recognition.

Special thanks to Brian McLemore, World Bible Translation Center's (www.wbtc.org) Vice President of Translations, who once again critiqued my efforts, and the result is a better book.

Anne White offered her expert advice and thoroughly critiqued this manuscript, even editing the endnotes for mistakes and errors. Her insights were invaluable to the final draft of this book.

Jay Stanwood once again gave me his common sense advice on how to reword obscure phrases. He challenged me to rethink difficult concepts. Rae Holt took his precious time to read the manuscript, point out difficult phrases, and offer important encouragement.

My good friends and team members, Rob Campbell and Steve Cordle, offered timely advice to make the final manuscript much better. I really appreciated the time they took to look over this book.

John and Mary Reith, as always, offered lots of encouragement and keen insight. Oliver Lutz gave me helpful suggestions and Gareth Hogg offered numerous suggestions and commentaries on this manuscript.

I appreciated Susan Osborn's expertise in copy-editing the final edition of this book.

Scott Boren, my chief editor, continues to do an incredible editing job. We've been together on twenty of my twenty-three books.

I also thank God for my wonderful wife, Celyce, for the listening ear and solid counsel she's given me throughout the process of writing this book.

Introduction

I was stunned when I understood the implications. A popular Christian author was saying that "spiritual Christians" will start their own "personalized churches," consisting of one individual only. He had redefined the word *church* to mean an individual watching a Christian TV show, going to a Christian concert, or home-schooling children. The author said that many spiritual Christians would leave the church in order to stay spiritual. And to justify this trend, he created a new category: individualized church. *This is the epitome of individualism,* I thought to myself. *Just perfect for a western, individualized culture.*

Although this author was promoting individualism for those leaving the church, many pastors and churches promote individualism for those attending the church.

Anonymity in the Church

I entered a famous mega-church a few years ago. I sat down for the service, didn't know those around me, and left the same way. But here was the catch: I wasn't supposed to know anyone. This particular church's appeal is anonymity and lack of "requirements." No membership requirements and no accountable relationships. I wandered outside and noticed a billboard highlighting only a handful of small groups.

This type of individualized, anonymous church experience is increasingly common throughout the Western world.

I initially grew as a new believer in this type of church environment. Many people, like me, gathered in masses to hear the Sunday preaching. The pastor was a gifted teacher and even though people could hear him on multiple radio stations, they still came to the preaching event.

Statistics now show us that an alarming number of "hearers" are leaving the church.

Yet, discipleship for the hearers totally depended on whether they could personally apply the teaching on a particular Sunday morning! Most attending weren't personally discipled. Granted, some discipleship groups sprang up naturally out of necessity, but the church didn't proactively plan for such discipleship to occur. God gave me the grace to apply the teaching and follow Jesus. Many weren't so fortunate and left the church.

Statistics now show us that an alarming number of "hearers" are leaving the church. Study after study highlights the reality that those "hearing" the Word in large group settings or via media are behaving the same way as those who don't listen at all.

David Olson, one of the premier researchers of the North American Church, in his book, *The American Church in Crisis*, goes into detail about the mass exodus taking place in the Church today. I believe this is partly due to the individualistic form of discipleship that is just not making disciples. We might be winning occasional battles, but overall we're losing the war.

The Way of the Master

The Bible never speaks of this individualistic form of discipleship. Jesus, our example, discipled twelve people by living with them for three years. He modeled discipleship as He lived, walked, and ate with them. He taught them through parables and real-life object lessons—not primarily in the large group setting.

Jesus didn't simply teach His disciples about prayer. Rather, He asked them to accompany Him to prayer meetings. He allowed His disciples to see Him praying. When the disciples finally asked Him what He was doing, He took the opportunity to teach them about prayer (Luke 11:1-4). The same is true with evangelism. Jesus evangelized people in the presence of His disciples and then instructed them afterwards. He took advantage of real life situations to carefully explain doctrinal issues (e.g., rich young ruler in Matthew 19:23-26).

Christ knew that theoretical information separated from practical experience would have little lasting value. After the disciples finished their ministry tour, they met with Jesus to discuss what happened. The apostles gathered around Him and reported all they had done and taught (Mark 6:30).

On another occasion the disciples reported to Jesus, "Lord, even the demons submit to us in Your name" (Luke 10:17). Jesus seized the opportunity to instruct them and to offer additional guidelines: "Do not rejoice that the spirits submit to you, but rejoice that your names are written in heaven" (Luke 10:20). The Lord constantly reviewed the experiences of His disciples and then offering additional commentary (Mark 9:17-29; 6:30-44).

The Early Church followed the same example. They applied the apostles teaching from house to house. They met publically as long as possible, but when persecution prevented public gatherings, they still continued to meet, moving from house to house (Acts 2:42-46).

The New Testament is written to communities, and discipleship takes place through relationships. Western individualism was absent from life in the First Century.

My Own Journey

I was born and raised in a Western, individualistic culture. Even though I spent eleven years of my life in Ecuador, I'm still a child of the West, and

I readily admit that I'm culturally conditioned to a particular way of thinking. I embraced Jesus in this culture and have been walking with Him for thirty-six years.

For most of my adult life, I was on the road to becoming a missionary. When I entered Bible school in 1978, I had missions in mind, so I took all the courses on cross-cultural ministry. Later in seminary, both in New York and Pasadena, culture was my bread and butter topic. As a missionary for eleven years in Ecuador, I was sensitive to the differences between my own Western culture and the Latin American culture.

I then earned a Ph.D. in intercultural studies. One of the Ph.D. tutorials was on Latin American culture. I inwardly resisted doing this tutorial, arguing to myself that I had over-studied culture already. Yet, the tutorial changed my life. It gave me an entirely new appreciation and insight into Latin culture.

Since returning from Ecuador in 2001 and becoming a "missionary" to North America, I've once again tried to become a student of culture. The study of culture has been a core part of my life and ministry.

While writing this book, however, I've noticed a subtle danger in my thinking about culture. The danger is to exalt culture to a place it doesn't deserve. I have this tendency. I find myself thinking, "That's just the way they are" or "That's the way we are." I tend to believe the lie that it's impossible to change one's culture because it's deeply embedded.

I've realized afresh that I need to judge my culture in light of God's inerrant Word. No culture is perfect, but God's Word is. Culture must conform to God's Word and not the other way around. I'm becoming increasingly aware that God desires to change me to conform to His Word. The Bible, not culture, needs to dictate all that I do and think.

Culture must conform to God's Word and not the other way around.

We in North America have developed a culture of individualism. While there are many wonderful traits of individualism, much of our present day individualism has led us down the dangerous path of isolationism, anonymity, and loneliness.

Biblical culture, on the other hand, is a one-another culture. Christ's command to His disciples is clear: Love one another. The Triune God is timeless testimony of God's unity. The Early Church was a face-to-face movement, meeting in homes and multiplying God's life through community.

This book has changed me. I've again realized that I need to conform to what God reveals in Scripture and allow the Holy Spirit to transform me into a relational disciple. That's what He wants, and I need to allow Him to work deeply within me.

My hope is that you will also be challenged and changed by reading this book. My prayer is that you will want to become a relational disciple, and that you will ask God for His abundant grace to transform you. You can't change yourself, but God can. God has promised His Holy Spirit to work deeply within you to make you a relational disciple.*

---

*This book is aimed at people in North America, but I also take the liberty to generalize about Western culture as a whole. When I use the term "the West," I'm referring to North America, Europe, and Australia.

Section One

Seeing Discipleship from a
Different Perspective

Chapter One

Conformed to the Pattern of Individualism

Bob Dylan wrote an award winning song in 1979 called, *Gotta Serve Somebody*. One line from the chorus reads:

"It may be the devil or it may be the Lord, but you're gonna have to serve somebody."

You're gonna have to serve somebody. This is true. Everyone is a disciple of someone or something. Some are disciples of liberalism, conservatism, or wealth. Others conform to Communism; others to Confucianism; others to Hinduism. It's impossible not to serve someone or something.

Without ever knowing it, we learn a way of living that shapes our way of thinking and relating. The word "disciple" simply means pupil or learner. In ancient times, a teacher's students or followers were called disciples. In the Greek world, philosophers were surrounded by their pupils. The Jews claimed to be disciples of Moses (John 9:28) and the followers of John the Baptist were known as his disciples (Mark 2:18; John 1:35). Jesus also had a group of disciples (Matthew 5:1; Luke 6:17; 19:37).

In Western culture, we are born into a culture of individualism. It's a philosophy that says:

"I can make it alone."
"I can do it by myself."
"I can pick myself up by my own bootstraps."
"I don't need help from anybody."

The Western world admires those who battle through difficult times and reach the top. We admire the hero who goes it alone. We see this in the cowboy of the West, Huckleberry Finn, and the Lone Ranger.

Yet, Paul the apostle warned the believers in Rome not to be conformed or shaped by the pattern of this world (Romans 12: 2). The Greek word Paul uses for *"conformed"* carries the idea of fashioning or becoming like someone or something. The world is constantly trying to fashion us according to its pattern, and Scripture tells us that we need to resist that conformity.

The Western World's Culture of Individualism

Alexis de Tocqueville, a French sociologist, wrote *Democracy in America* (1835) after his travels in the United States. Even today, his writings on American culture speak truth. He described individualism in North America this way:

Individualism is a calm and considered feeling which disposes each citizen to isolate himself from the mass of his fellows and withdraw into the circle of family and friends; with this little society formed to his taste, he gladly leaves the greater society to look after itself.[1]

The Western world admires those who battle through difficult times and reach the top.

While de Tocqueville admired American individualism, he also noticed the grave danger of isolationism that could easily capture the hearts of Americans. He writes:

As democratic individualism grows, there are more and more people who, though neither rich nor powerful enough to have much hold over others, have gained or kept enough wealth and enough understanding to look after their own needs. Such folk owe no man anything and hardly expect anything from anybody. They form the habit of thinking of themselves in isolation and imagine that they hold destiny in their hands.[2]

De Tocqueville felt isolationism could be a real problem for Americans. He hoped that civic and social responsibility would bring people together to meet in groups and prevent Americans from developing their own cocoons.

Isolationism is the result of individualism separated from the triune God. It has increasingly evolved into immorality and family breakdown.

One hundred seventy-five years have passed since de Tocqueville visited these shores. I wonder what he would think now.

Isolationism and loneliness are now part of the American psyche. Anxiety, loneliness, mood disorders, and social detachment are now common place. More and more people are depressed. George Gallup wrote, "Americans are among the loneliest people in the world."[3]

M. Scott Peck says:

> Trapped in our tradition of rugged individualism, we are an extraordinarily lonely people. So lonely, in fact, that many cannot even acknowledge their loneliness to themselves, much less to others. Look at the sad, frozen faces all around you and search in vain for the souls hidden behind masks of makeup, masks of pretense, masks of composure.[4]

Isolationism is the result of individualism separated from the triune God. It has increasingly evolved into immorality and family breakdown. It's estimated that six out of ten children born in the 1990s will live in single-parent households by the time they're eighteen years old.[5]

Individual achievement in and of itself is good. God wants us to use the gifts and talents He's given us to the highest level possible. The fact is, however, that individualism causes us to isolate ourselves from others and focus only on what benefits "me"— fulfilling Tocqueville worst fears.

Individualism and Others

People's lives are more and more centered inside the house, rather than in the neighborhood or the community. It's common for people to drive into their driveways, go into their houses, and seldom interact with the community around them.

Walking has decreased significantly in America to a point in which it's rare to meet others outside. With the increased use of automobiles, the life of the sidewalk and the front yard has largely disappeared, and social intercourse that used to be the main characteristic of urban life has vanished.

In 1974 nearly one in four Americans visited with a neighbor several times a week. By 1994, that figure had declined to 16 percent and there was a shocking increase in the number of people who had never spent an evening with a neighbor—a 41 percent increase since the same question was asked twenty years earlier.[6]

I remember attending a barbeque at the home association where I live. People just hung out by themselves. They didn't reach out, and I found it hard to make bridges into their lives. I was amazed at how lonely people could be in a group setting.

John, one of our church members, volunteered to coach his boy's baseball team. His hope was to get to know others and develop relationships with them. He found out, however, that parents would

---

Moving is also an American way of life. The statistics say that one in five Americans move each year.

---

come to the baseball diamond and quickly pick up their kids. They wouldn't hang around to talk.

Are people less relationally inclined today because they have less time? Actually, people still have about the same amount of leisure time as they did during the World War II period. The key factor, rather, is what people are doing with their leisure time. Between 1965 and 1995 Americans gained an average of six hours a week in leisure time, and yet, almost all six of those additional hours were spent watching TV.[7]

Harvard professor, Robert Putman, in his book, *Bowling Alone*, describes the downward spiral of social relationship in North American culture from the end of World War II to the present. The title of Putnam's book is revealing. Bowling used to be the sport that drew people together. Bowling was associated with friends, family, or the development of new social relationships. Bowling is now a lone venture. Another isolated activity.[8]

On the Move

I understand moving. As a missionary family to Ecuador for eleven years, we often lived out of our suitcase, as we traveled from North America to South America.

Moving is also an American way of life. The statistics say that one in five Americans move each year. Two in five expect to move in the next five years.[9] We as Americans have an itch to see different sites and hear new sounds. I spoke to a friend who was a long-term member of a church in San Diego. She told me that her church has been riddled with people moving. It had become a revolving door. Her experience is not uncommon.

Increased mobility, however, has decreased long-term relationships. Americans don't get to know their neighbors very well. Will Miller and Glenn Spark, in their book, *Refrigerator Rights*, warn people about the huge social price tag that comes with relocating. Often, they say, right at the point of deepening their friendships with neighbors and colleagues, they move to another city, and the process of developing friendships has to start all over again. They've noticed that fewer people in North America feel like they have the liberty to enter someone's home, open the refrigerator door, and make a sandwich. This lack of "refrigerator rights" is often due to the high mobility of American society.

Relationships take time to develop. They don't happen overnight. It takes awhile to earn the trust of a neighbor or work associate. Whenever we move, we're moving away from the people we know. It's difficult to replace those relationships.

I remember eating with Buddy Lindsay in a fish restaurant in Myrtle Beach, South Carolina. Buddy is a tax lawyer in Myrtle Beach, was raised in Myrtle Beach, and likely will die there. As I talked with Buddy that sunny day in February, I realized that he personally knew the majority of business owners and key people in the city. *This guy understands community*, I thought to myself. People know, love, and respect Buddy because he's taken the time to get to know them. Buddy is a great example of blooming where he was planted.

My parents have also lived in the same house in Long Beach, California since 1950. My mom organized her neighborhood to have regular block socials. She has always been involved in PTA, Assistance League, and other social activities. Even at eighty-three she is still giving back. Most of us can think of these kinds of wonderful examples, but it appears that they are increasingly becoming exceptions to the rule.

Media Isolation

TV has changed the world. We can now virtually travel to places in an instant, learn insights about history and science, and enjoy a good laugh together. And when the NBA championships roll around each year, I love TV.

TV is so popular, in fact, that the average American watches four hours of it each day.[10] This is nearly the highest viewership in the world. The average U.S. household has at least one TV set turned on for about seven hours a day. The average school-aged child spends twenty-seven hours per week watching TV (some preschoolers watch much more). Television absorbed almost 40 percent of the average American's free time in 1997, an increase of roughly one-third since 1965. Over the course of a year, children spend more time watching TV than they spend in school or participating in any other activity, except sleep.

The TV is molding who we are. It is socializing us. Years ago, TV watching was done in a group. The entire family would sit before the TV and enjoy the same program. It is much different today. Viewers sit before the tube all by themselves. Many households have a TV in each room in order to accommodate personal viewing preferences.

One of the key reasons TVs are hanging in exercise rooms around the country is because they allow people to avoid engagement in social dialogue. Many unconsciously believe that watching TV gives them a "relationship with the TV person," so they think they're engaged socially, when in fact they are not. TV also keeps people from buying books and reading.

Even a relational sport, like bowling, is now invaded by TV. Robert Putnam writes:

> Even on a full night of league play team members are no longer in lively conversation with one another about the day's events, public and private. Instead each stares silently at the screen while awaiting his or her turn. Even while bowling together, they are watching alone.[11]

TV is in airports, bars, hotels, stores, and restaurants.

TV is often the babysitter of choice for those with children. Wrong move. Studies show that TV watching has three main effects on children: they become less sensitive to the pain and suffering of others, they become more fearful of the world around them, and they are more likely to behave in aggressive and harmful ways.[12]

TV has drawn people to isolation in their house. Time diaries show that husbands and wives watch TV three or four times more than they spend talking to each other, and six to seven times as much as they spend in community activities outside the home.[13]

The Church Mirrors Society

Church congregations are made up of the same people who live in society. Kirk Hadaway, author and professor, touches this raw nerve when he writes, "Churches like society itself have become more and more impersonal. It is not enough to hear it from the pulpit, read it in the Bible, or see it in individuals. It has to be experienced in community."[14] The Spirit of God transforms people, and transformation takes place in community.

Like the transitory nature of the greater society, statistics say that one in seven adults change churches each year. People often decide on which church to attend based on personal taste and choice. Mark Galli, senior managing editor of *Christianity Today*, writes:

> . . . our penchant for changing churches, usually because "I just wasn't being fed," as well as our need to test every church and pastor against our personal reading of the Bible—well, you can see why Protestants have managed in 500 years to create out of two traditions (Orthodox and Catholic) some 30,000 denominations. . . . the personal experience of the worshiper so often becomes more important than the object of worship. Thus, the continual proliferation of churches, parachurches, and movements because the group we belong to just doesn't do it the way we

think "the Lord is leading me" to do it.[15]

Many churches use marketing and other techniques to attract those wandering from church to church. Rather than making disciples who make disciples, marketing becomes the chief means to draw people into the building. In their book, *Selling Out the Church: The Dangers of Church Marketing*, Philip Kenneson and James Street noted that the entrepreneurial church is "viewed primarily as a business."[16]

Marketing the church using marketing principles may not necessarily be wrong, but one needs to ask, "Can the market-driven church remain Christ's church?"[17] Once again, Scripture, rather than culture must guide all we do or say. Jesus is interested in growing an organic, life-giving church, rather than an anonymous and impersonal one.

It's easier to criticize than provide solutions. Often believers in the church see themselves as individuals first, Americans second, and Christians third. Those in the church are the same people who appreciate their rights, freedoms, and independence. These are the same people who don't know their neighbors next door, much less trust them.

Getting Back to Relational Discipleship

God desires for us to be dependent on Him and interdependent with one another. Community is about the people of God working together, eating together, and serving together. Jesus has called us to live out the Christian faith. We are social creatures, and our Creator has placed within us a longing for relationships.

One encouraging sign is that the upcoming generations are more relational. The post-modern culture desires authentic communication with people. They are saying, "We don't want to do church without loving relationships."

Younger people in general are far more open to community and relationships than their predecessors. The emerging church is hungry for Christ-like relationships and reality-based ministry. They want to see Jesus in people before they're ready to "decide" for Jesus. Generation Next longs for a relational form of church—one that views ministry in terms of relationally-based New Testament ministry rather than techniques and programs that a supposed to make the church grow.

Chapter Two

Transformed by the Trinity

I have to admit, I never thought the Trinity had much personal application. The Trinity seemed like a nice theological concept but nothing more. I studied it in college, mentioned the Trinity in sermons, and of course, believed it. But a concept that might transform me? No way.

My views have changed radically. Lately, I've found myself meditating in wonder and complete amazement. Here are some of my thoughts:

I love and serve a God who exists in perfect relationship.

God is not a lone-ranger. He exists in community.

His communion with the other members of the Godhead is my model to follow.

I'm excited about God's nature. He's a relational God. He's not an individualist. He desires community.

And then my excitement deepens when I realize that this triune God lives within me. He's molding and shaping me from within to become a relational disciple. The Trinity resides in every believer--Father, Son, and Holy Spirit. God's very nature, therefore, is to guide His children to form relationships with others.

God's relational nature pours out from the pages of the Bible. Notice how many times Scripture talks about community, love, and close relationship among His people. These Scriptures simply reflect God's character.

God Himself is the One doing the transforming, and His goal is to mold us into His image.

As mentioned in the last chapter, the culture of this world is trying to "conform" us to its values. Paul also uses the word "transformed" in Romans 12:2. He tells us not to be conformed to the world but to be transformed by the renewing of our minds. We get our English word "metamorphous" from this word "transformed." It refers to a total change from the inside out, rather than from the outside in.

God Himself is the One doing the transforming, and His goal is to mold us into His image, as He says in Genesis 1:26, "Let us make man in our image, in our likeness. . ." Notice, the plurality of "let us" and "our image." God is transforming us into His own image, which is relational.

Larry Crabb writes:

> We were designed by our Trinitarian God (who is Himself a group of three persons in profound relationship

with each other) to live in relationship. Without it, we die. It's that simple. Without a community where we know, explore, discover, and touch one another, we experience isolation and despair that drive us in wrong directions that corrupt our efforts to live meaningfully and to love well.[18]

What Is the Trinity?

You won't find the word Trinity in the Bible. Scripture is abundantly clear, however, that there is only one God, and that all three persons (Father, Son, and Holy Spirit) are called God. The Bible teaches that:

- The Father is God: "yet for us there is but one God, the Father, from whom all things came and for whom we live" (1 Corinthians 8:6).
- Jesus is God: "But about the Son he says, 'Your throne, O God, will last forever and ever'" (Hebrews 1:8).
- The Holy Spirit is God: Then Peter said, "Ananias, how is it that Satan has so filled your heart that you have lied to the Holy Spirit . . . You have not lied to men but to God" (Acts 5:3-4)
- There is only one God: " Hear, O Israel: The LORD our God, the LORD is one" (Deuteronomy 6:4).

One famous early church creed, the Athanasian Creed, describes the Trinity this way:

> For there is one Person of the Father: another of the Son: and another of the Holy Ghost. But the Godhead of the Father, of the Son, and of the Holy Ghost, is all one: the Glory equal, the Majesty coeternal. Such as the Father is: such is the Son: and such is the Holy Ghost.

For me, the clearest statement is simply that there is one God, eternally existing in three persons: Father, Son (Jesus Christ), and Holy Spirit.

The truth is that we can't fully explain the Trinity. God is infinitely greater than we are, and we can't completely understand Him.

Because of our limitations, illustrations have been used to describe the Trinity. Some are better than others. A widely used illustration is the triangle. One triangle has three corners, which are inseparable from, and simultaneous to, one another. In this sense it is a good illustration of the Trinity. Of course, the triangle is finite and God is infinite.

Augustine, the early church scholar, illustrated the Trinity from 1 John 4:16, which tells us that God is love. Augustine reasoned that love involves a lover, a beloved, and a spirit of love between lover and loved. The Father might be likened to the lover; the Son to the one loved, and the Holy Spirit is the Spirit of love. Yet love does not exist unless these three are united as one. This illustration has the advantage of being personal, since it involves love, a characteristic that flows only from persons.

The Trinity and Community

Have you ever been in a group in which you felt a clash of personalities? Perhaps one person tried to dominate the conversation. Perhaps you came face-to-face with a quirky personality that turned you off. When you're ready to act in an ungodly response (e.g., lashing out, gossip, anger), ask God to help you to act like the Trinity. Instead of demanding personal attention, ask God for strength to walk in humility, while praying for the person.

Jesus often pointed to the unity within the Trinity as a model for His disciples to follow. Notice how Jesus describes His relationship to the Father:

> That all of them may be one, Father, just as you are in me and I am in you. May they also be in us so that the world may believe that you have sent me. I have given them the glory that you gave me, that they may be one as we are one (John 17:21-22).

The unity of the Father, Son, and Holy Spirit jump out from the pages of Scripture. The New Testament reads like a living love letter between the triune God and His people:

- The Father loves and delights in the Son (Matthew 3:17).

- Jesus receives the love of the Father and pleases Him out of love and obedience (Matthew 12:31). Jesus says, "When a man believes in me, he does not believe in me only, but in the one who sent me. When he looks at me, he sees the one who sent me" (John 12:44-45).
- The Spirit glorifies both the Father and the Son (John 16:14). The Spirit's job is to bring back to memory the Words of Christ (John 16:12-15).

Each person of the Trinity loves, honors, and glorifies the other and receives love and honor back from the others. Jürgen Moltmann, a famous theologian, wrote:

> The three divine persons are not there simply for themselves. They are there in that they are there for one another. They are persons in social relationship. The Father can be called Father only in relationship with the Son; the Son can be called Son only in relationship with the Father. The Spirit is the breath of the one who speaks.[19]

We are supposed to imitate God's relational nature. Christ gathered twelve disciples and journeyed with them for three years to demonstrate and teach them about love and community. Their lives molded and shaped together was the key component of their training.

Jesus had a huge challenge to unite such a diverse group. He brought together disciples who were temperamental and easily offended. They often saw each other as competitors. It wasn't easy for them to wash each other's feet (John 13:14).

Each person of the Trinity loves, honors, and glorifies the other and receives love and honor back from the others.

Jesus continually taught the importance of unity and love for one another. He told them that people outside the fold would recognize they were His disciples by the love they had for one another. He even said that the world would believe when they saw the unity the disciples showed toward one another. Jesus prayed to the Father, "May they be brought to complete unity to let the world know that you sent me and have loved them even as you have loved me" (John 17:23).

The writers of the New Testament didn't stop talking about community. The phrase "one another" appears one hundred times in the New Testament and most of those occurrences have to do with relationships between believers and how to cultivate those relationships. The next chapter focuses on the "one anothers."

The Trinity Working in Us

How many times have we promised by our own strength to do something and failed? So many times we've made promises like:

"I'm going to practice the golden rule."
"I will love my enemy because God says to."
"I will love my neighbor."

The bottom line is that apart from the Spirit of God working through us, we can't fulfill the one anothers of Scripture.

We suffer from an individualistic, dog-eat-dog mentality. We are determined not to submit to anyone. The harmony and love within the Trinity is so distinct from our own human natures that He has to transform us with that same love for community to happen.

Moving from a life of individualism toward one of community requires a powerful inner transformation. God does it through us, and it flows out to others.

I love personal devotions and even wrote a book concerning them.[20] Yet, more and more I understand that personal devotions are not really personal. Rather a time of personal devotion is communion with the Trinity, the three in one. Devotions are all about growing in a love relationship with a God who does not act independently or in a selfish, individualistic manner. Our relationship with Him then overflows to our relationship with others.

During a quiet time, you catch a glimpse of what perfect love and unity is all about. After spending time in His presence, we can see others through His eyes. Dietrich Bonhoeffer experienced the horrors of Nazi Germany, the embodiment of human-centered pride. Yet, in the midst of such chaos, Bonhoeffer wrote, *Life Together*, a treatise of God-centered community between believers. He writes:

> The believer therefore lauds the Creator, the Redeemer, God, Father, Son, and Holy Spirit, for the bodily presence of a brother. The prisoner, the sick person, the Christian in exile sees in the companionship of a fellow Christian a physical sign of the gracious presence of the triune God. [21]

God helps us see His presence in others and to love them like He does. He transforms us to act like Him. Acting independently goes against His character. Community, in fact, is the very nature of God.

Our goal should be to yield to the Spirit and allow Him to mold and shape us. As we do, He will stir us to love one another, serve one another, wait on one-another, walk in humility with one-another, and to fulfill the one-another commands in the Bible. Speaking of the believer's freedom, the Apostle Paul states "nobody should seek his own good, but the good of others" (1 Cor. 10:24).

Chapter Three

Transformed by One Another

Mary Franciscus, a good friend and member of our church, was driving down the narrow road from Lake Havasu on a hot summer day when her right front tire ripped apart. The car skidded and swerved into the opposite lane. As she looked up, she saw an SUV approaching from the other direction. Fearing for her life and the little ones in the car, she desperately jerked her car to the right, pulling back into her lane and barely missing the SUV that barreled by. She pulled over, the car skidded to a stop, and everyone sighed with relief.

But what was she going to do in the 110 degree heat, far from her husband Humphrey's help?

Before she could call 911, she turned around to see three marines walking toward her. On the back window of their car was a bumper sticker, "Not of this world."

"Can we help?" they said. "Thanks so much," Mary blurted out. *Is all this really happening?* she thought.

The three men changed the tire and even checked the brakes.

She then asked if she could pray for them, knowing they were on their way to Afghanistan. They nodded in agreement.

Later in the car, Mary said to her kids, "God had a purpose in all this. God wanted me to pray for them."

I can imagine the Marines getting back in their car and saying, "She really needed us. God wanted us to help her."

And they needed each other. Mary required the helping hand for her car and the Marines needed prayer for their service in Afghanistan.

We need each other. The term in the Bible for "one another" is a reciprocal pronoun meaning "mutual ministry."

The triune God is a model of community. God desires that the love relationship between members of the Trinity transforms His Church.

Focusing on Others

I've tried to create categories that make the biblically based one-anothers more easily understood. One broad category is to focus on others, rather than on oneself.

We naturally focus on our own needs and wants. Someone said that when you're fifteen years old, you are concerned about what others think about you. When you're forty-five, you really don't care what people think about you. When you're sixty-five, you realize that no one was thinking about you anyway! The truth is that we spend most of our time thinking about ourselves. Paul said, "For everyone looks out for his own interests, not those of Jesus Christ" (Philippians 2:21). The triune God longs to guide us to focus on others.

Love one Another

We are taught from a young age to rise to the top, as a rock climber might scale a precipice. "Make it on your own" is a well-known refrain. While personal achievement is not wrong, Jesus asks us to make sure we're not stepping over others in the process.

Christ's mandate to the disciples superseded personal achievement. He told them to highlight the interest of others over their own personal interest. He said to them, "A new command I give you: Love one another. As I have loved you, so you must love one another. By this all men will know that you are my disciples, if you love one another" (John 13:34-35).

The context of these verses is Jesus washing the feet of His disciples. Christ's command was straight forward: do what I'm demonstrating. Such love was revolutionary in those days, just as it is in our day.

Serve one Another

The disciples were a lot like us. They had visions of personal grandeur and success. Two of the disciples walked up to Jesus, asking to occupy positions of power in the kingdom (Mark 10:37ff).

The two were willing to leapfrog over the other disciples, if necessary. They asked, "Let one of us sit at your right and the other at your left in your glory." Notice the response of the other ten disciples, "When the ten heard about this, they became indignant with James and John" (Mark 10:41).

According to Jesus, the greatest disciples are those who reach down to make others successful.

I was reminded of a scene in the movie "Yes Man," in which Jim Carey tries to land an executive position, only to find more than one hundred unemployed ex-executives clawing, striving, and viciously competing for one opening. Trying to climb over others to make it to the top always breeds indignation, envy, and competition.

The mentality of many is, "Do whatever it takes to climb to the top, even if it means walking over others on the way there." Christ responded to the two disciples saying:

> You know that those who are regarded as rulers of the Gentiles lord it over them, and their high officials exercise authority over them. Not so with you. Instead, whoever wants to become great among you must be your servant, and whoever wants to be first must be slave of all. For

> even the Son of Man did not come to be
> served, but to serve, and to give his life as
> a ransom for many (Mark 10:42-45).

According to Jesus, the greatest disciples are those who reach down to make others successful. They are empowered with God's Spirit to serve others before themselves. This is such a contrast to our own selfish desires that it requires a new nature to make it work.

And God readily supplies supernatural love to those who ask. Paul says:

> For Christ's love compels us, . . . And he
> died for all, that those who live should
> no longer live for themselves but for him
> who died for them and was raised again
> (2 Corinthians 5:14).

As God's love flows through us, we are empowered to serve others and to look not only on our own interests but of those of others (Philippians 2:4).

Forgive Each Other

"Real men get even." At least that's the perception reinforced by many Hollywood movies. In such movies, the actor launches off on a personal crusade to kill all those who have wronged him. Real life, of course, is much different. Often, offended people get even by withdrawing. They stop talking. Stop communicating. Leave. Many marriages end up in this manner, filled with bitterness for years to come.

What's true in the world is also observed in churches. Churches are filled with hurting, difficult people. Jesus tells us to forgive each other. Membership is often like a rotating door of congregants from one church to another. And the reasons for leaving often have to do with disliking the pastor, problems with a board member, or being overlooked to lead a program. So people leave, hoping the problems won't appear in the next church.

Jesus tells us not to be bitter and resent others. The way forward is through forgiveness. This doesn't mean ignoring problems, but it does mean that whether or not others make godly responses to our appeals or confrontations, we still need to forgive. Of course, none of us have the power to forgive; therefore, we need His grace and power to forgive. He did say He would give us strength if we asked (Matthew 7:7).

I dealt with one believer who left a church and held deep bitterness against the pastor. The pastor said to me, "It's like he's drinking the poison he hopes will kill me." *So true*, I thought.

Paul is writing to the church when he says in Colossians 3:13, "Forgive as the Lord forgave you." Author Mike Mason writes:

> If you want to be free, set others free.
> Give everybody lots of rope, even if they
> try to use it to hang you. To love people

is to enjoy them truly, warts and all. Give everyone the freedom to be imperfect.[22]

Build Up Each Other

It's so easy to use gossip to tear people down. I remember one church member who loved to talk about her great accomplishments while gossiping about the shortcomings of others. Although she had many wonderful traits (e.g., diligence, relational skills), her words were like a whirlwind, wreaking havoc on those in her path. I had to confront her on more than one occasion and was concerned about what her actions would be at the next church she attended.

Writing to the church, Paul says, "So then we pursue the things which make for peace and the building up of one another" (Romans 14:19). We are Christ's body on the earth, and we need to lift each other up by speaking truth to each other.

The phrase "build-up" in the Greek literally means to reconstruct each other's lives (oikodomeo). All of us have areas that need renewal and repair. Jesus uses fellow believers as messengers to speak into our lives. It's often hard to be willing to receive correction from others, but this is an important part of becoming Christ's disciple.

Paul said to the Romans, "I long to see you so that I may impart to you some spiritual gift to make you strong" (1:12). Yet, in the next sentence he says, ". . . that is, that you and I may be mutually encouraged by each other's faith." We need each other and our spiritual gifts come to life as we minister to one another in the body of Christ.

Encourage Each Other

When Peter denied Jesus three times, I wonder if Peter entertained the idea of ending it all in his state of hopelessness. But Peter wasn't alone in his despair. The other disciples had also denied they knew Jesus. Peter turned to them in his grief, and they all rejoiced together when they saw the resurrected Christ.

Rugged individualists glory in self-sufficiency. Yet, the reality is that humans are frail. We can't do it on our own. None of us are so capable and confident that we don't need and appreciate being encouraged.

Life has a way of beating us down and making us feel that we just don't quite measure up. Dan Blazer writes in *The Depression Epidemic*:

> Many of us are subject to sometimes dehumanizing corporate or economic systems not of our making and seemingly beyond our influence. We feel small, insignificant, and expendable.[23]

The impersonal nature of this world tends to suck the life from us. We feel dehumanized and mechanical. Encouragement refreshes us. It reminds us that God has a purpose and plan for our lives. We're encouraged to press on. Hebrews 10:25 says, "Let us not give up meeting together, as some are in the habit of doing, but let us encourage one another–and all the more as you see the Day approaching."

Jesus is coming soon. But until that moment, we need to press on in the face of doubt, and discouragement. God-inspired encouragement, like a bridge, helps us to pass over dark depression and uncertainty and get to the other side. Paul says, "Therefore encourage one another and build each other up, just as in fact you are doing" (1 Thessalonians 5:11).

Be Kind to One Another

Secretly showing kindness to someone doesn't make headlines as a Billy Graham event, a best-selling Christian book, or a concert of a famous Christian band does.

Yet, God sees caring acts of love and kindness done for His glory. Hebrews 6:10 says, "God is not unjust; he will not forget your work and the love you have shown him as you have helped his people and continue to help them."

Kindness is the practice of being sympathetic and compassionate. It's an act that shows consideration and caring. Paul tells us to "Be kind and compassionate to one another . . ." (Ephesians 4:32). The world attaches weakness to such kindness, but when Christ controls a believer, the fruit is kindness, compassion, and sympathy toward others.

My mother lightens up all those around her. Her gift of service and kindness is unmatched.

She doesn't simply tell people she loves them, she shows it. People like to be around Phyllis Comiskey because she's so generous. She can't go by a garage sale without thinking of my kids. My mother makes my kids, and everyone else around her, feel special and cared for through her acts of kindness. John the apostle writes:

> Dear children, let us not love with words or tongue but with actions and in truth. This then is how we know that we belong to the truth, and how we set our hearts at rest in his presence whenever our hearts condemn us. For God is greater than our hearts, and he knows everything (1 John 3:18-20).

Mike Mason highlights the promise of confidence in 1 John 3:19-20 by saying, ". . . I've learned the power of small deeds of kindness for lifting depression. Kindness lifts depression because it strikes at the root of depression, which is self condemnation."[24]

Christians began many of the world's great social programs. The founders were believers who simply wanted to reach out in Christ's name through humble and selfless acts of kindness. You show kindness in simple ways: giving up your seat on a crowded bus, offering your jacket, cooking a special meal, offering a ride, or helping place a carry-on in the overhead bin.

Be Devoted to One Another

When Jesus enters our hearts, our lives are transformed, and we are given a completely new nature.

My conversion to Christ thirty-six years ago was an amazing, supernatural event. God has also been working another conversion in my heart. It's a conversion to one another. Paul says in Romans 12:10, "Be devoted to one another in brotherly love." The word "devoted" might be translated "kindly affectioned." Paul had the devotion of a family in mind.

Those in the church are part of a heavenly family, joined together by Jesus Christ Himself. Devotion to one another implies we won't run when life is difficult. It's a commitment that we shouldn't take lightly.

Accountability

None of us are lone-rangers on this journey in Christ's kingdom. Rather, we are fellow travelers on the same heavenly-bound journey. Scripture tells us to look out for one another and hold each other accountable.

Instruct One Another

Frank lived with a woman for years while attending the Sunday morning services in an evangelical church. No one asked him about his arrangement with the woman. Most likely no one even knew about it. One Sunday when he was at church, I invited him to the small group at my house, which I led. He accepted the invitation and became a regular member of the group. His lifestyle soon became apparent. He couldn't hide. The people in the group began to minister to Frank.

Sometimes we depend too much on the "preacher" to do the work of the church. Paul believed that all Christians were ministers.

God's Word through others began to convict Frank's heart that he should either marry or break-up. Frank agreed to separate from his live-in partner, while they decided what to do. They eventually married, entered our discipleship training, and became leaders of a small group.

Scripture tells us that we are God's instruments to instruct each other. Paul says, "And concerning you, my brethren, I myself also am convinced that you yourselves are full of goodness, filled with all knowledge and able also to admonish one another" (Romans 15:14). Paul was writing to a house church, in which everyone knew each other. Paul wanted the believers to know that they were the ministers. God had equipped them to speak into each other's lives and counsel one another. Sometimes we depend too much on the "preacher" to do the work of the church. Paul believed that all Christians were ministers.

The best way to instruct one another is through God's Word. Paul says in Colossians 3:16:

> Let the word of Christ richly dwell within you, with all wisdom teaching and admonishing one another with psalms and hymns and spiritual songs, singing with thankfulness in your hearts to God.

My wife and three daughters recently journeyed to Panama on a mission trip. Together they had to raise eight thousand dollars in three months. Upon hearing this, one person said, "That's impossible." My wife politely "admonished" this person saying, The Bible says, "What is impossible with men is possible with God" (Luke 18:27). God empowered Celyce and my daughters to raise all eight thousand dollars before leaving. The person who doubted now likes to tell the story about the time his own unbelief confronted the truth of God's Word. God's Word won, of course.

Submit to One Another

Submission is a rarely spoken word in a modern, politically correct culture. Independent, free-thinking, and even rebellious people are prized and esteemed. Biblical truth, however, surpasses what people prize. And Scripture tells us to submit to one another. Paul says in Ephesians 5:21, "Submit to one another out of reverence for Christ." Paul writes this verse immediately before talking about husband and wife relationships.

Husbands are quick to point out the need for wives to submit. Yet, Paul tells husbands, wives, and the church at large to submit to one another. Mike Mason says:

> In fact, the essential way we are to submit to God is by submitting to one another. A certain religiosity may cause us to humble ourselves before God. But unless we also humble ourselves before people, we are fooling ourselves. Relationships with people are the litmus test of our holiness.[25]

The church of Jesus Christ is called to submit to one another.

Confess Sins to One Another

God recently showed me how to resolve a troubling issue in my own life. He then revealed that I needed to be more transparent about the issue and to ask for prayer. When I shared it with others, they also became transparent about their own problems.

We all have struggles. We are on a journey, and God's love and grace encourage honesty with one another. Deitrich Bonhoeffer writes:

> You can hide nothing from God. The mask you wear before men will do you no good before Him. He wants to see you as you are. He wants to be gracious

to you. You do not have to go on lying
to yourself and your brothers, as if you
were without sin; you can dare to be a
sinner. Thank God for that. He loves the
sinner, but He hates the sin. All shame
was ended in the presence of Christ.
Community is a place where people can
be vulnerable and transparent. [26]

God powerfully worked in the lives of the youth at
our church after they came back from a conference.
God changed them at the event, but the fire kept on
burning through the times of confession and prayer
within the group as the weeks and months wore
on. One person in particular was gut-level honest
about his sins and failings. He was the spark that
ignited others to share about their struggles.

Confession of sin and praying for one another
has always been a part of revivals around the world.
Superficiality, though, is the enemy of revival.
Bonhoeffer continues:

Now he stands in the fellowship of a
sinner who lives by the grace of God in
the cross of Jesus Christ. Now he can
be a sinner and still enjoy the grace of
God. He can confess his sins and in this
very act find fellowship for the first time.
The sin concealed separated him from
the fellowship, made all his apparent
fellowship a sham; the sin confessed has
helped him to find true fellowship with
the brethren in Jesus Christ.[27]

Interdependence

Our sinful nature tends to exalt self before others. Scripture tells us that we need to look upon our brothers and sisters as more important than ourselves. This is a supernatural activity because we are naturally born selfish. Paul the apostle says:

> I hope in the Lord Jesus to send Timothy to you soon, that I also may be cheered when I receive news about you. I have no one else like him, who takes a genuine interest in your welfare. For everyone looks out for his own interests, not those of Jesus Christ (Philippians 2:19-21).

It requires a supernatural work of grace to go beyond our own selfishness and think about the needs of others.

Walk in Humility with One Another

Have you ever been in a group in which everyone wanted to be the center of attention? Did you notice that people weren't really listening? Or that everyone wanted to talk at the same time?

We long for the spotlight. We crave the attention, credit, and esteem of people. The problem is that everyone wants the same thing.

True servants of Jesus are willing to humble themselves, deny the spotlight, and esteem others better than themselves. Peter says, "Clothe yourselves with humility toward one another, for God is opposed to the proud but gives grace to the humble" (1 Peter 5:5). God's plan is for us to walk humbly, give up our own rights, and allow others to be lifted up. True humility is a work of God's grace within. There's nothing in us that desires humility or longs for it. Yet the Trinity desires to perfect this characteristic in us.

Accept One Another

Christ's church is made up of imperfect people with many needs. His church is mocked by the world's version of high society—the in group. In comparison, the church of Jesus Christ is a hospital, full of broken, hurting people. And because we are all saved and accepted by God's grace, we must accept all those in Christ's family. Larry Crabb writes:

> I don't need to keep up my guard. I can actually accept you as God for Christ's sake has already accepted me. When you offend me, I can nourish the spirit of forgiveness within me because it's there. I may have to look hard for it, but it's there. I've been forgiven, and I've been given the urge to forgive, the same urge that led to my being forgiven. I can pour into you the life that has been poured into me. [28]

Jesus accepted me when I was opposed to Him, living in rebellion. The Bible even says that while we were enemies of God, He reconciled us to Himself (Romans 5:10) and made us alive when we were dead in sin (Ephesians 2:5). Because no one is part of God's church because of personal merit or righteousness, God calls us to accept all those who He has accepted, in spite of the differences. Paul says in Romans 15:7, "Accept one another, then, just as Christ accepted you, in order to bring praise to God." The basis for accepting others as they are is the fact that God has accepted us just as we are. Paul tells us that God has chosen the foolish and despised to bring glory to Himself:

> But God chose the foolish things of the world to shame the wise; God chose the weak things of the world to shame the strong. He chose the lowly things of this world and the despised things—and the things that are not—to nullify the things that are so that no one may boast before him (1 Corinthians 1:27-29).

True disciples of Christ accept people as they are, with all their fears, weaknesses, ethnic differences, and backgrounds. As with the other relational truths of Scripture, we need the power of the Holy Spirit to actually put this one into practice. Mason says:

> If I want to know true fellowship with others, the first step is the same: to make a decision to join my heart with theirs.

Then together we ask Jesus to come into the one new heart that has been formed between us.[29]

Live at Peace with One Another

The early believers often faced conflict. Families were ripped apart due to persecution. Believers sometimes met underground, away from the watchful eyes of the Roman Empire. Jesus, knowing the believers would face persecution, said to them, "I have told you these things, so that in me you may have peace. In this world you will have trouble. But take heart! I have overcome the world" (John 16:33). Peace in times of persecution is a necessity.

Living at peace with others means accepting people the way God has made them and forgiving their faults.

Peace is also needed in the middle of inter-personal strife. Envy, jealousy, and bitterness can so easily cloud our relationships with one another. The Early Church had to carefully guard against the pettiness that comes with human conflict. Paul exhorted the believers to "Live in peace with one another" (1 Thessalonians 5:13b).

Living at peace with others means accepting people the way God has made them and forgiving their faults. Speaking the truth in love to people is a prerequisite for living at peace. Avoidance of gossip is a sure remedy for strife and turmoil.

Bear with Each Other

The majority of Western culture is now indoctrinated with evolutionary teaching. This theory promotes the survival of the fittest, which supposedly is how certain species survive and others perish. The natural conclusion of evolution is that the strong survive, and the weak perish. Hitler's Germany was an extreme example of such teaching.

Scripture tells us that God created all people equal. The weak are just as important as the strong. God tells us to bear with the weak to uplift them. Paul says:

> We who are strong ought to bear with the failings of the weak and not to please ourselves. Each of us should please his neighbor for his good, to build him up. For even Christ did not please himself but, as it is written: "The insults of those who insult you have fallen on me" (Romans 15:1-3).

And then in another passage, Paul writes, "Carry each other's burdens, and in this way you will fulfill the law of Christ" (Galatians 6:2).

Jesus didn't pass by the blind and the afflicted on His way to fellowship with those in high positions. Rather, he spent more time with those who had needs and burdens. He healed the blind and gave food to the hungry. He fulfilled Isaiah's prophesy:

> The Spirit of the Lord is on me, because he has anointed me to preach good news to the poor. He has sent me to proclaim freedom for the prisoners and recovery of sight for the blind, to release the oppressed, to proclaim the year of the Lord's favor (Luke 4:18-19).

Jesus demonstrated for us the need to bear with the weak and helpless. We can't bear the burdens of others if our primary relationship with them is just on Sunday morning. We need to get close to people to hear their hearts, know their needs, and bear their burdens.

Wait for One Another

David Shi, a cultural historian, writes about the inability to slow down in America. Waiting is intolerable. We work endlessly and press on against all odds. Edward Stewart says:

> The foreign visitor in the United States quickly gains an impression of life lived at a fast pace and of people incessantly active. This image reflects that doing is the dominant activity for Americans. The implicit assumption that "getting things done" is worthwhile is seldom questioned.[30]

Waiting is practically anathema in a hurried and rushed world. Paul's exhortation to the Corinthians is timely in our day and age: "So then, my brothers, when you come together to eat, wait for each other. If anyone is hungry, he should eat at home, so that when you meet together it may not result in judgment" (1 Corinthians 11:33). Waiting on others is difficult, so we need God's strength to make it happen. All things are possible!

Like the Corinthians, we often lack the self-discipline and patience to wait for others. We need to hear Paul's exhortation to allow Christ to form His character in us, which places others above ourselves and highlights the discipline of waiting on one another.

Honor One Another

In the Early Church, it wasn't uncommon for slaves to be leading the house church meetings, while the masters would intently listen. Such is the nature of the body of Christ, in which all members are important—both men and women. In ancient culture, women were considered to be inferior to men. Yet Paul says:

> You are all sons of God through faith in Christ Jesus, for all of you who were baptized into Christ have clothed yourselves with Christ. There is neither Jew nor Greek, slave nor free, male nor female, for you are all one in Christ

Jesus. If you belong to Christ, then you are Abraham's seed, and heirs according to the promise (Galatians 3:26-29).

Christ envisioned a church in which all members had the same care and honor for each other. Paul says in Romans 12:10, "Honor one another above yourselves." This is the beauty of Christ's body in that even the lowliest receive honor and equal standing.

To honor Jesus means honoring the Christ who lives in every believer. Each member of the body of Christ is a chosen child of the King who will live forever with the Master. If we honor the Master, we must also honor those who He has chosen.

Use Your Gift among Each Other

Many have been hurt by worldliness in the church, which leads them to say, "I don't need organized religion." And I would agree that we don't need organized religion. But we do need Christ's supernatural, organic body in which He empowers its members to use their gifts to minister to one another.

The gifts are not an impersonal phenomenon that people do alone. God gifts His people to minister to one another. Each time the gift passages are highlighted, the New Testament writers use body terminology. Gifts, in other words, function reciprocally. Each part of the body plays a role in both giving and receiving.

Every born-again believer has at least one gift. Peter says:

> Each one should use whatever gift he has received to serve others, faithfully administering God's grace in its various forms. If anyone speaks, he should do it as one speaking the very words of God. If anyone serves, he should do it with the strength God provides, so that in all things God may be praised through Jesus Christ. To him be the glory and the power forever and ever (1 Peter 4:10-11).

Whether you have a speaking gift (e.g., teaching, pastoring, prophesy) or a service gift (e.g., mercy, helping, giving), God desires for you to discover it and manage it well.

God distributes the gifts to build up and empower His church. This is why God placed the "love chapter" (1 Corinthians 13) between the two key chapters about the gifts of the Spirit (1 Corinthians 12 and 14). The motivation for using God's gifts is to strengthen others in the faith—never to show off or to impress others.

Show Hospitality to One Another

We planted our church in Moreno Valley, California, using our house as the launching pad. I struggled with the constant barrage of people in our home and the resulting messiness. I found it hard to practice hospitality and was on my knees a lot, asking God for patience and grace to deal with certain people. God continually had to remind me that my home and possessions are not my own. They belong to Him, and He wants to use them to bless others.

When I have shared these struggles with others, I've found that I'm not alone. One of the greatest hindrances to small group ministry is the lack of hospitality.

In New Testament times, the homes of the believers served as both church building and hotel for traveling preachers and ministers. Hospitality was a necessity. With urgency Peters says, "Offer hospitality to one another without grumbling" (1 Peter 4:9).

In today's society, hospitality is becoming a lost art. People are often possessed by their possessions, insist on their personal time, and open their homes less and less. God is calling relational disciples to open their hearts and homes to others.

Things have a tendency to possess us. We start focusing on the things rather than the purpose for them. When God graciously gives a nice home to a believer, it's to use in the service of others.

Watchfulness

Most of the one-another verses are positive. Yet, Scripture also warns believers against the invasion of the sinful nature. And this nature, like the devil himself, is prone to kill, steal, and destroy (John 10: 10). God calls relational disciples to reflect His character, avoiding the opposite tendencies.

Do Not Lie to Each Other

Bernard Madoff was convicted of operating a Ponzi scheme that was the largest investor fraud ever committed by a single person (reportedly almost sixty-five billion dollars in fabricated gain). On June 29, 2009, he was sentenced to one hundred fifty years in prison.

It's hard to comprehend how Bernard Madoff could swindle billions of dollars from friends, family, and investors while knowing all that time that he was stealing their money. Perhaps Madoff felt a certain exhilaration and power in impressing people with his money-making scheme. I guess we'll never know.

Our new nature discovers total fulfillment and self-worth in Jesus, where there's no need to lie and deceive.

Like Madoff, our sinful nature is consumed with projecting a certain image to impress people. Our new nature, in contrast, discovers total fulfillment and self-worth in Jesus, where there's no need to lie and deceive. Jesus said in John 3:20-21:

> Everyone who does evil hates the light, and will not come into the light for fear that his deeds will be exposed. But whoever lives by the truth comes into the light, so that it may be seen plainly that

what he has done has been done through God.

Those who come into the light know they can't hide anything from an ever-present God. It's impossible. And because we can't hide from God, it's useless to try to hide things from one another. In Colossians 3:9 Paul says, "Do not lie to each other, since you have taken off your old self with its practices."

Light and lies don't mix. Lies seek darkness. Truth lives in the light. And Scripture calls believers the children of the light. We no longer are in darkness because Christ has set us free.

Do Not Fight with Each Other

Before speaking in a conference in Belfast, I had the chance to tour the streets. Graffiti marked buildings and bunkers that set apart the Catholic and Protestant sectors of the city.

Only now is healing returning to that war-torn part of the world. Paul says, "If you keep on biting and devouring each other, watch out or you will be destroyed by each other" (Galatians 5:15).

Strife and conflict create more turmoil. Bitterness leads to more bitterness. Paul tells the church to stop it. Resist biting and devouring one another and let love reign. Paul gives this advice to his spiritual son Timothy:

> And the Lord's servant must not quarrel;
> instead, he must be kind to everyone,

able to teach, not resentful. Those who oppose him he must gently instruct, in the hope that God will grant them repentance leading them to a knowledge of the truth, and that they will come to their senses and escape from the trap of the devil, who has taken them captive to do his will (2 Timothy 2:24-26).

As believers, we're not immune to the vicious cycle of "biting and devouring." Yet, as we grow in Christ, we realize how unproductive it is to give way to anger and bitterness. Relational disciples know that God is not honored by hatred, so they choose to follow the path of peace and love.

Do Not Envy One Another

Envy is part of the sinful nature list of Galatians 5:19-21. Envy is often a secret sin that eats away at the soul. Paul tells believers to choose another path: "Let us not become conceited, provoking and envying each other" (Galatians 5:26). Often we become envious when we forget God sets members in His body as He pleases. When we forget this fact, we start comparing ourselves with others, wanting gifts and positions outside God's will.

The Holy Spirit desires to give us a generous spirit that esteems other people. The prayer of the believer is, "Lord, free me from envy and help me to esteem others." Only Christ in us can give us the power to truly esteem others, turning envy into honor and respect.

How refreshing when a believer resists envy and builds up others. My brother Jay is like that. My mom and I joke about Jay saying, "Jay doesn't have a jealous bone in his body." Jay is always building others up. He always seems to have the best interests of the other person in mind.

Do Not Judge One Another

C.S. Lewis once said that pride is putting down others to make ourselves look good. Pride, in other words, shows itself when we judge others. The thought process is, "I'm actually doing pretty good in comparison with so-and-so." Paul tells believers to take the higher road saying, "Therefore let us stop passing judgment on one another. Instead, make up your mind not to put any stumbling block or obstacle in your brother's way" (Romans 14:13).

I was in one church recently in which I felt God's love throughout the congregation.

As I spent time with the church leadership, I realized that a key value they displayed was the refusal to tear others down and the commitment to speak positively about others. The uplifting atmosphere of the church drew people like a magnet, and Jesus was ultimately glorified.

People already receive enough criticism, both from their own conscience and those around them. The world, the flesh, and the devil major on belittling others. Paul says:

> Therefore judge nothing before the appointed time; wait till the Lord comes. He will bring to light what is hidden in darkness and will expose the motives of men's hearts. At that time each will receive his praise from God (1 Corinthians 4:5).

Judgment belongs to God. Only He knows and sees the entire story. We are so limited in what we know and perceive that it's far better to leave judgment in His hands, knowing He will reveal all things in His time.

God's Empowerment

Although we live in this world, we are part of another one. The new world order is radically different than this one. It follows different rules and guidelines.

The good news is that God fills us with the Holy Spirit to make the Bible clear to us. And just as importantly, He gives us the power to fulfill what the Bible teaches.

One of the ways in which God transforms us is through conflict. I believe that God allows conflict in our lives to forge love and community with one another. It's quite easy to sing songs about love, service, and humility. It's quite another story to practice these disciplines in the middle of a battle, when every emotion screams no way. In the next chapter, we'll look at how God molds us into relational disciples through conflict.

Chapter Four

Transformed by Conflict

In 2001, I led a small group that I felt was going very well. My wife and I were growing in our relationship with another couple who were coming to our church. Yet, the husband was having problems with me, and I didn't know it.

One day the husband announced that he was leaving the small group because of personal issues with me. I admired his candor, honesty, and boldness to tell me what he was thinking. At the same time I was emotionally crushed because I didn't have a chance to make amends, learn from my mistakes, and resolve the situation.

I felt pain and hurt in his departure, not because he had an issue with me, but because I wasn't able to work through the issue with him. He didn't give me the opportunity to change, improve, and grow as a person. He just left.

As I grappled with the situation, God showed me that true community involves working through problems and confronting issues. We grow the most when we openly communicate with one another, receive guidance, make mid-course changes, and continue to grow in the relationship.

God works through conflict to transform His disciples. He uses it to mold and shape us. Conflict with our brothers and sisters tests our Christian character and ultimately forces us to our knees, asking for the Holy Spirit's help. In such times, we discover our need for God, knowing that we can't love and forgive anyone apart from His powerful working within us.

I remember one preacher saying, "Do you want to learn to love someone?" Have a conflict. It's in the realm of people conflict that our love is tested. Being connected with God is the easy part. After all it's by grace through faith. The harder step is connecting with people.

It seems easier to run from problems, but running won't solve them.

Do Not Run

Conflict often arises as we clash with different personalities and character deficiencies—often the very character deficiencies that annoy us are ones that we share, but sometimes don't recognize. We might see anger, impatience, gossip, unfaithfulness, and personality quirks. When we come up against such problems, the tendency is to run or ignore the problem. Most of us have known people who never quite work through their relational problems. They run from one broken relationship to the next.

Jill (not her real name) was like that. Before coming to Christ, she was deeply depressed and tried to commit suicide several times. Jesus changed Jill's life, and she made great progress, but problems continued to linger.

She struggled to communicate with others and had a tendency to blame people for her own deficiencies. Problems were always someone else's fault. I knew Jill's tendency but thought the relationship between our families was different.

Then we clashed. Problems occurred that should have been resolved. I tried several times to reconcile. No deal. She quickly packed up and left emotionally, and eventually left the church.

I've often thought about why she reacted the way she did. Maybe her withdrawal was a defense mechanism to keep her from further hurt? She employed this method with her mentally challenged mother, so it came naturally.

Jesus is still working on Jill, and the story isn't finished. He desires to enter the deep recesses of her heart and bring true healing.

It seems easier to run from problems, but running won't solve them. Often people hop from church to church to avoid the pain of dealing with relational conflict. As soon as they're known by the pastor and the people, they conveniently slip out to another church.

I counsel people not to run to a different church with unresolved pain and troubles. It's best to stay put and allow God to work within the person. Mike Mason writes:

> Lovelessness often results from an inability to confront others in a healthy way. There is a time, place and manner for confrontation, but most of us shy away from this important work and so end up simmering in quiet rage.[31]

Avoidance is never the answer. Jesus molds us through the personality difficulties we face. And yes, we will face them.

Care Enough to Confront

A few years ago, I attended a large conference in Indonesia. I wasn't one of the speakers. The organizer of the event told me I'd have a chance to announce my new ministry called *Cell Church Solutions*. I met with the organizer for breakfast and thought he would give me a chance to say a few words. At least that was the plan. I was disappointed when he didn't ask me to come forward. Rather, he mockingly said, "Oh yea, Joel has a new ministry called *Cell Church Solutions*. So sign up in the back if you're interested. I guess Joel has all the solutions. Ha ha."

Two things caused me to react strongly. First, he didn't allow me to make the announcement. I had hoped to personally greet the people at the conference. Second, he jokingly made a sarcastic remark about my new ministry.

What was my reaction? Anger! I stayed in my room that night and didn't go to the evening celebration. I was hurt deeply. I cut off fellowship with others by hiding in my room, when I should have talked directly to the person right away. I often think about my behavior at that event and use it as incentive not to repeat such immaturity.

I did talk to that person, but it was two years later! And he received what I had to say with loving acceptance, saying, "I joke way too much and need to be more sensitive to others. I'm truly sorry and please always feel free to talk with me." We became close friends as a result of open communication and have even become partners in several ventures.

I have learned my lesson with this brother. I promptly talk to him whenever there's a conflict, and he's equally ready to talk to me. We've grown as disciples through conflict!

People often separate caring from confronting: Caring is good, confronting is bad. David Augsberger, however, thinks the two go together. He's coined the word care-fronting. Augsberger says:

> Care-fronting is offering genuine caring that bids another grow...Care-fronting is offering real confrontation that calls out new insight and understanding...Care-fronting unites love and power. Care-fronting unifies concern for relationship with concerns for goals. So one can have something to stand for (goals) as well as someone to stand with (relationship) without sacrificing one of the other, or collapsing one into another.[32]

Most people live by the maxim, "Avoid conflict whenever possible." But conflict and disagreement will happen no matter what people do or how well they do it. A Chinese proverb declares, "The diamond cannot be polished without friction, nor the man perfected without trials."

Holding back and being "nice" when you should share the truth does not serve the person's best interests. Ephesians 4:15 says, "Instead, speaking the truth in love, we will in all things grow up into him who is the Head, that is, Christ."

Relational conflicts often force us into God's presence as nothing else will. We become highly dependent on Him through these trials. I remember my own experience as a missionary in Ecuador. I found myself emotionally and spiritually gasping for air at times due to relational conflict with other missionaries. I'm sure they felt the same way because I wasn't very sensitive. Yet, through it all, I matured as a missionary and grew as Christ's disciple.

Forgive Those Who Offend You

Embittered people are everywhere. They might be next door neighbors, work associates, or family members. They are typically good people who have worked hard at something important, such as a job, relationship, or activity. When something unexpectedly awful happens--they don't get the promotion, their spouse files for divorce, or they fail to make the Olympic team--a profound sense of injustice overtakes them. Instead of dealing with the loss with the help of family and friends, they cannot let go of the feeling of being victimized. Almost immediately after the traumatic event, they become angry, pessimistic, and antagonistic.

Life-engulfing bitterness never comes overnight. It starts small and grows. Before it becomes a consuming habit, it's entertained on a smaller scale. But bitterness, fed by demonic forces, never intends to stay small. It desires to possess its victims and eventually control them.

If anyone deserved to hold bitterness, it was Joseph. Joseph had to work through the death of his mother (Genesis 35:19), and also face his brothers' hatred (Genesis 37:4). They tried to kill him but ended up selling him to a band of slave traders who were on their way to Egypt. If that wasn't enough, in Egypt Joseph was again betrayed—this time by the wife of the master of the house. She accused him of adultery (Genesis 39:14-15). He languished in prison due to this false accusation. Then in prison, Pharaoh's principal official promised to help him get out (Genesis 39–40). That hope was again crushed by the official's forgetfulness.

Through all the pain and suffering, Joseph kept his focus on God's love and grace. He never allowed his heart to become hard. And through Joseph's trials, God had a plan. He lifted up Joseph to become second in command to Pharaoh (Genesis 41). The key lesson that we can learn about Joseph is that he never allowed the venom of bitterness to poison his life.

When God lifted Joseph up, he could freely lead and give of himself. Just like Joseph, we live in a sinful and unjust world, full of pain, abandonment, abuse, fear, prejudices, discrimination, hurt, loneliness, rejection, resentment, and anger.

You might be struggling with those who have wronged you. But remember the words of Jesus, "And when you stand praying, if you hold anything against anyone, forgive him, so that your Father in heaven may forgive you your sins" (Mark 11:25). The way to avoid habit-forming resentment is to reject it immediately.

The way to avoid habit-forming resentment is to reject it immediately.

In 1985 when I was the pastor of a new church plant called Hope Alliance, I desperately longed for affirmation when I was struggling. One day I received a phone call from Anne, one of the members. I figured she needed counseling or prayer. I was shocked when Anne directed her complaints against me, telling me that I was a failure, that no one liked me, and that it was best to find another profession. Her words cut deep into my sensitive soul. The hurt soon turned into bitterness. I was filled with resentment the next day as I drove from Long Beach, California to Fresno, California to attend an Evangelism Explosion conference. I remember dwelling on her words during that long, restless drive. Right outside Fresno the bitterness reached a boiling point. I stopped the car and cried out to God.

At that moment I heard God clearly whisper, "Joel, if you're not willing to forgive Anne, neither will I forgive you your sins." I opened my Bible and read these words of Jesus, "For if you forgive men when they sin against you, your heavenly Father will also forgive you. But if you do not forgive men their sins, your Father will not forgive your sins" (Matthew. 6:14). I wrestled with God. *How could I forgive this woman who wronged me and wounded me so deeply?* Yet, I also recognized that I couldn't live life filled with bitterness. God won that afternoon. He filled me with His love, power, and forgiveness. He gave me the grace to forgive.

When I returned to Long Beach, I discovered that Anne was a deeply wounded person and her remarks reflected that hurt. Often we don't know why people react and hurt us. But God still calls us to forgive.

It's now fourteen years since God called me to forgive Anne, but He's still teaching me to forgive. Recently my wife and I were discussing our roles in marriage, and she revealed that she felt I was pressuring her. We talked it through, and she had a good cry. But then I started feeling bitter. *She made my day miserable,* I thought. *Why did she even have to tell me that I was putting pressure on her?* Self-justification and bitterness began to well up within me. I should have rejected it immediately, but I allowed it to fester. I found myself in an emotional straight jacket. *But she put me there,* I shot back. *I'll get back at her.*

That evening, I went for a long run. God spoke clearly to me. He showed me that it was my fault. I confessed my bitterness to God, His blood cleansed me, and His refreshing peace flowed through me. I came home from the run, gave my wife a hug and kiss, and we continued in close fellowship.

I tend to clobber people with unforgiveness. I'd prefer to stay mad because it makes me feel justified. *That person wronged me, and I'm not going to let him or her off the hook so quickly,* I say to myself. Then God gets hold of me, reminding me Peter's words, "Above all, love each other deeply, because love covers over a multitude of sins." (1 Peter 4:7-8). The word "deeply" in Greek literally means to "stretch out." It denotes the tense muscle activity of an athlete.

Forgiving others often requires the stretching and exercising muscles we didn't know existed. I've discovered through experience that only the Holy Spirit can empower a person to cover over the sins of others through forgiveness. This type of love doesn't come naturally--only supernaturally. Bitterness and revenge are natural instincts.

We need to ask the Holy Spirit to transform us, giving Him the freedom to reveal the areas of life in which we need healing. We need to believe that God will give us the power to forgive people who have caused us sorrow and pain.

The good news is that as we receive the forgiveness of Christ, He gives us the strength to forgive others. Scripture says this about Jesus: "But he was pierced for our transgressions, he was crushed for our iniquities; the punishment that brought us peace was upon him, and by his wounds we are healed" (Isaiah 53:5). Receive forgiveness and then release that person who has offended you.

Larry Crabb says:

> We must be equally quick to teach that with the atonement there is forgiveness, with forgiveness there is connection, and with connection there is the community of faith, a community destined to enter the bliss of perfect connection forever. The point of the whole plan is relationship, a connected community.[33]

Jesus offers a crown of beauty instead of ashes, the oil of gladness instead of mourning, a garment of praise instead of a spirit of depression (Isaiah 61:3). Jesus wants to lift that burden from us.

Rebuild Trust

I served in a church in which a key pastor committed a moral failure that drove dozens and dozens from the church. This pastor confessed his sin to the church, and I continued to work with him.

My new relationship with him, however, was different. I didn't have the same trust and confidence in him, because I wondered if it could happen again. Before his fall, I was impressed when he freely shared his spiritual dryness and lack of time with God. After his fall, I became concerned when he shared such things. My trust barometer had gone way down.

Forgiveness and trust are not the same. Trust often takes time to rebuild. Trust is not always restored, but we must always forgive. A friend of mine was hurt deeply by his boss (and close friend) who asked him to leave suddenly. I counseled my friend not to hold bitterness, knowing that he would be the one destroyed. I was glad when he wrote back:

> I know this and have actively forgiven
> ____. I am praying for my hurt to catch
> up with my confession and believe me
> I am doing much better. For me to
> go back to the relationship as it was is
> not possible. Not because of the issue
> of forgiveness, but one of trust. I am
> doing my best before God to move ahead
> without bitterness, anger, or malice, and
> I think I have done that. I could not
> stand in unforgiveness and bitterness
> and expect God to lead me into the
> future. Forgiveness doesn't mean things
> will be as they were. It means that I have
> released those hurts and feelings to the
> Lord and in the process he will bring
> healing.

Knowing when you have forgiven a person is a tough question that is not easily answered. But it does not mean forgetting the offense. It's practically impossible to forget memories of past hurts.

Forgiveness, rather, is measured by whether you actively take pleasure in the bad feelings that comes from that memory. If someone has hurt you, you need to release that person each time the bad memory comes to your mind. And more than likely you frequently will recall this painful moment. Not just once or twice. Anne's offense popped into my mind many times after I forgave her, but I remembered my commitment to release her.

Forgiving and Forgiven

Becoming a relational disciple involves forgiving others, but it also means asking others to forgive you. Proverbs 6:2–5 says:

> If you have been trapped by what you said, ensnared by the words of your mouth, then do this, my son, to free yourself, since you have fallen into your neighbor's hands: Go and humble yourself; press your plea with your neighbor! Allow no sleep to your eyes, no slumber to your eyelids. Free yourself, like a gazelle from the hand of the hunter, like a bird from the snare of the fowler.

If you've blown it and you know it, don't allow your pride to tell you it doesn't matter. No. Go to the person who you have offended and ask for forgiveness. Jesus said:

> But I tell you that anyone who is angry with his brother will be subject to judgment. .... Therefore, if you are offering your gift at the altar and there remember that your brother has something against you, leave your gift there in front of the altar. First go and be reconciled to your brother, then come and offer your gift" (Matthew 5:22–24).

Even if your brother doesn't choose to forgive you, you can be confident that you have been forgiven by God, and you have done what God has asked you to do.

God wants to bless us through this process. He wants to free us from the hurt and bitterness that come with unforgiveness. Forgiveness is a source of blessing not only for the other person but for us as well.

Scripture is clear that God wants to mold us into relational disciples. But what does that look like practically? In the next section, I'll attempt to answer that question.

Section Two

Practicing Relational Discipleship

Chapter Five

Practicing Relational Discipleship with the Inner Circle

I watched on TV the divorce announcement of a high profile husband and wife pastoral/ preaching team. They told their church that they were getting a divorce, but that they would continue ministering as usual. He would continue pastoring the church, but she would move to another state to lead her already established para-church ministry.

They are acting as if nothing happened, I thought to myself. *Have we descended into such an abyss that our Christianity does not work at the most intimate levels of our lives?*

I can imagine that some in the congregation felt justification when they heard the news that morning. After all, those who were in church that morning had most likely experienced divorce at the same rate as those who weren't attending. Mark Galli writes:

> The rate at which evangelicals divorce is hard to distinguish from the larger culture's, and the list of reasons for divorce seems no different: "'We grew apart.'" "'We no longer met each other's needs.'" "'Irreconcilable differences.'" The language of divorce is usually about the lack of self-fulfillment.[34]

One of the saddest things about Western culture is the breakdown between the personal and public lives of people. It is acceptable to say, "I don't care what he or she does in private. That's none of my business."

God cares.

He's not interested in public success without private victory. The two go hand in hand. In fact, Christ prioritized teaching twelve disciples for three years, so that they might later pass the "multitude test." He wanted those few to successfully "flesh out" His Words in daily life and action.

True success is having those closest to you love and respect you the most.

By concentrating on them, He would eventually reach the multitude. But He needed to focus on quality first. The quality would bring the quantity. Christ's intentional concentration on the twelve gains significance by knowing that the multitudes wanted to take Him by force and crown Him King (John 6:15). Even the Pharisees admitted that the world had gone after Him (John 12:19).

Christ is also concerned about relational success with those who we are closest to, the ones who know us best. If we have not been molded by the iron sharpening iron process of those who see us up close, the holes in our souls will eventually be exposed.

In the next chapter we'll cover the small group or micro church. As the circle widens from there, it then embraces the local church and finally the mission circle.

Those Closest to You

I was attending a Promise Keeper's rally back in July 1996, when I first heard John Maxwell talk about true success. He said, "True success is having those closest to you love and respect you the most."

Maxwell's recipe for success came from Christ's playbook: Start with the inner circle and grow from there.

When I heard Maxwell utter these words, I didn't catch the full weight of what he said that afternoon, but over the years, I've had time to reflect on life, ministry, and relationships. Maxwell's words have convicted me to prioritize what really matters in life.

And even though community involves many areas of our lives, the most important community relationships are those closest to us. If community doesn't work there, it really doesn't work.

Who are those closest to you? Only you can answer that question, depending on where you are in life.

If you're married, I believe your spouse is number one on your list. If you're a child, it's your parents, brothers, sisters, and close friends. If you're divorced with kids, those closest to you would be your children. If you're a university student, perhaps your inner circle would be a fellow believer you meet with regularly.

If you don't have an inner circle, ask Jesus to help you form one. He will direct you to one or more people with whom you can have a close friendship and accountability relationship.

I believe God first uses the community in the inner circle to mold and shape His disciples. It's with these people that we first successfully practice the one-anothers, growing through conflict, and the other concepts discussed in this book.

Some are eager to start with the crowd. They yearn to be in front of people. God's plan, however, is to start small. God molds His disciples through those who have more intimate knowledge of their lives and ministry.

Priorities

I have the privilege of speaking to crowds around the world. Those who I meet for the first time don't know me personally. Perhaps they've read one of my books, and hopefully I've given them a good impression while speaking. Yet, they don't know the real me. And I don't know them.

My wife and family, however, know me intimately. They see Joel Comiskey up close and know how successfully my faith translates into the nitty-gritty of life. They witness how I deal with real-life circumstances. Living the Christian life, rather than talking about it, becomes essential with those who I'm closest with. Words take a backseat to action and lifestyle.

God's work of grace starts with the inner circle. It's in that circle that I receive criticism, gain true encouragement, and make mid-course corrections. As I pass the inner circle test, God can then use me in greater spheres of influence.

Spouse

The first link in my inner circle is my relationship with Celyce. I married her on February 13, 1988. She knows how I react to life's circumstances. She knows the *why* behind my life and ministry, and her counsel is based on patterns and experiences that only she knows. God also uses me to sharpen her.

My desire is to be the best husband possible and to develop the deepest, most intimate relationship with Celyce. She's not a part of my ministry. She is my ministry.

I'm saddened to think that during certain periods in our marriage I acted as if the main goal in my life was personal success and that marriage was designed for my own good. I expected her to "fall in line" and help me in my ministry. God has slowly, graciously shown me that Celyce is my number one ministry. The chief questions I have to ask are:

- Does she feel we're improving in our marriage?
- Are we having fun together?

- Am I spending quality time with her?
- Are we growing in our friendship?
- Am I sensitive to seeing things through her eyes?

We have to diligently work on our relationship. Conflict can spring up at anytime. In fact, conflict is a key part of the disciple-making package, as we learned in the last chapter. The intensity of marriage brings those conflicts to a new level.

In marriage, we're both learning to ask God to give us the grace to say, "I'm sorry," confess our own sin, and then move on. We rejoice that our love and relationship is growing deeper all the time.

God might be using your spouse to drive you to your knees. You might have to ask God for grace and forgiveness. Believe that God is molding and shaping you.

The truth is that tragedies strike families and marriages all the time. The good news is that God rebuilds inner circles.

Some of you reading this book have experienced a broken inner circle through divorce, death, or some other tragedy. God is able to start the process over and give you a new inner circle. You might have failed in your relationship with your children, behaved badly toward your parents, or disassociated with close friends. No matter what the situation, God's grace is sufficient and He loves to reshape lives.

Mario, a friend of mine, was a successful pastor in Long Island, New York. His church grew quite large. Then his inner circle began to unravel. His wife, diagnosed with bipolar disease, began having an intimate relationship with another woman.

Mario tried everything to save his marriage, including months of counseling under the watchful eye of his Baptist superintendent. His wife continued to pursue her lesbian relationship and eventually divorced Mario.

He was then asked to leave the church. You can imagine the depths of darkness Mario faced at that time. Thankfully, his children, seeing their dad's godly responses throughout the crisis, remained faithful to Jesus.

Eventually Mario remarried Nancy, a beautiful Christ-like woman, and began working in the secular world. His call to the ministry tugged at his heart, and years later he answered God's call to return to the pastorate.

I was thrilled to hear that an evangelical church in Texas hired Mario, after examining his rebuilt inner world. The church saw how God had used his tragedy to make him stronger.

I've been in contact now with Mario on a regular basis. He has a deeper compassion for people. He's walked with God through the valley and has come out stronger and wiser. He's able to help others through difficult times because God has helped him.

The truth is that tragedies strike families and marriages all the time. The good news is that God rebuilds inner circles, like He did with Mario. Christ can completely turn a dark situation into a shining example.

God is the God of hope. He loves to display His strength in weakness and failure. He wants to make you a relational disciple who will have an impact on the lives of many.

Family

I remember eating with one missionary who told me that his dad, an international minister, stopped his ministry for one year to spend time with him during his troubled years. I admire this father's commitment to place the well-being of his child above his own ministerial success. Sadly, many have not. They've placed their own success in life over their relationship with their children.

As I travel around the world, I often meet parents who are mourning one or more children who are no longer following Jesus. I certainly don't condemn them. While writing this book, my kids are eighteen, fifteen, and thirteen. I'm excited to say that they are on-fire for Jesus and serving Him, but I'm on my knees asking for God to continue to work in their lives.

Spiritual Growth

I believe the highest goal for our children is that they would love the Lord God with all of their heart, soul, and strength. This is my greatest desire for my children. I want to make sure I accurately pass the baton of the Christian faith to them, and that they would remain radical disciples of Christ.

To help ensure this happens, I've led devotions with my kids almost every day since my oldest was three years old. I've adapted my devotional style as they've matured. Our normal devotional time includes taking time to worship, pray, and wait in silence for Jesus to speak to us. Afterwards, I ask each of them to share what God showed them. I then share what God has shown me from the Word, trying to speak on their level. As they have grown older, they share in our devotional time what God showed them in their own personal devotions.

I'm surprised that some parents don't take the time to develop their kids spiritually. They don't lead spiritually. They leave the spiritual leadership to the youth leader, Sunday school teacher, or someone else. They also grieve when their children lose their spiritual moorings due to youth pressures. I urge parents to prioritize the development of spirituality in their children.

God uses parents to equip children to hear God's voice and follow Him. I'm convinced that the family quiet time is the best time for parents to nurture children in the ways of God and really prepare them for life with Christ.

Growing godly, healthy kids isn't only about shared devotional time. It's also about friendship, fun, and spontaneous activity. Plato once wrote, "You can learn more about a man in an hour of play than in a year of conversation."[35]

We've also found that a twenty-four hour day off is essential--both for parents and family members. It solidifies so many things. It gives the family a chance to have fun, gather strength, and face the upcoming week with new vigor. It helps the family build and maintain strong relationships.

Be Real

I'm constantly reminded that my kids are God's instruments to make me more like Jesus. God uses them in the discipleship process. Michael Ferris, an educator and author who successfully raised three daughters, wrote a book called *What a Daughter Needs from Her Dad.* He says:

> From a very early age your daughter will know when you have made the wrong decision, snapped to an inappropriate judgment. . . A father who refuses to admit a mistake or work at changing poor, immature behavior reaps a daughter who refuses to trust him. . . . Your reliability is actually enhanced when you are willing to admit to the evident fact that you have made a mistake.[36]

My constant prayer is that I would admit my mistakes when my children point them out. It's a far better choice and builds respect. I've acted so immature at times, bursting out in anger, behaving impatiently, and not being sensitive. When this happens, I've found it far better to humble myself, apologize, listen to my kids, and then ask God to work deeply within me. God wants to mold me through these situations.

A Secure Environment

Children feel cared for and loved when the husband and wife live in harmony. We know through experience that when we as husband and wife are doing well, our children feel secure. When I make my wife feel special, my kids honor me in a special way. I believe a successful relationship between husband and wife is half the battle when it comes to child-rearing. The husband and wife relationship is the glue that makes the other relationships work. The greatest thing a father can do for his children is to love his wife.

One Christian friend who suffered a divorce recently recalled his son asking during the divorce proceedings, "Where is God in all this, Dad?" The son still hasn't recovered. The glue of marriage, which was supposed to help this boy grow in his relationship with God, unraveled. One reason why God hates divorce is because the children suffer in the process. Malachi says:

> Has not the LORD made them one? In flesh and spirit they are his. And why one? Because he was seeking godly offspring. So guard yourself in your spirit, and do not break faith with the wife of your youth. "I hate divorce," says the LORD God of Israel, "and I hate a man's covering himself with violence as well as with his garment," says the LORD Almighty. So guard yourself in your spirit, and do not break faith (Malachi 2:13-16).

God is looking for godly offspring as parents prioritize each other and their children. God desires for kids to see community lived out between father and mother. When this is not the case, insecurity develops. Often bitterness surfaces toward the parents because of the vague hopelessness the child feels about his or her own prospects in developing close relationships with friends and a future spouse. Inconsistent parents birth insecure children.

My heart's desire is that we as parents would wholeheartedly make our inner circle our first priority.

Friends

Jesus made friendships a top priority. He enjoyed going to the home of Mary, Martha, and Lazarus. This was probably a place where Jesus could relax and feel like a normal human being.

Christ's disciples were also His friends. Jesus had a special relationship with John. We all need a best friend, one who we can share intimate details of our lives.

Spouses need additional friendships outside of the marriage.

Friendship was also important to Paul the apostle. Notice what he says in 2 Corinthians 2:12-13:

> Now when I went to Troas to preach the gospel of Christ and found that the Lord had opened a door for me, I still had no peace of mind, because I did not find my brother Titus there. So I said good-bye to them and went on to Macedonia.

Although preaching the gospel was very important to Paul, he saw friendship as essential.

The authors of *Refrigerator Rights* feel that too many people look to their spouses to fulfill all their emotional needs, putting a tremendous strain on the marriage. Spouses need additional friendships outside the marriage.

I was recently in Hong Kong doing a seminar. Afterwards I toured the city with a group from Japan. I hung out with Doug, a career missionary to Japan who married a national. We talked about his unique training ministry around the world. As we walked he said:

> As I speak to leaders within Japan and in other countries, the one common denominator is the lack of friendship. Busy leaders are often very lonely. They have few people to turn to in times of need.

We both acknowledged that it's not just a leadership problem. It's a problem we all face. In the Western culture especially, we consume our extra time with work and don't take time for friendships.

My advice is to find one or two solid friends of the same gender to talk to and share with. Open your heart and schedule to those people—both fun, spontaneous time as well as serious sharing time.

Friendship is not a one-way street. People, who only want to talk and not to ask questions and listen, don't make good friends. Kevin Strong is one of my best friends. Kevin does two things really well. First, he shares what's happening in his life. He doesn't hold back. He talks about things as they really are. Second, Kevin asks great questions. He practices active listening (e.g., "so I hear you saying. . . .) and he asks additional questions to draw out meaning.

Establish regular contact with your friends. Have fun together. Play sports. Practice self-disclosure. One of the key ingredients of a true friend is transparency. Dave is a great friend. I admire the way Dave maintains past and present friendship by calling, hanging out, and making time for one-on-one moments. And he's also very transparent. He's always willing to share his struggles.

We are all on a journey. We all face physical, emotional, and spiritual struggles. It's great to have someone with whom you can share those struggles. A friend is someone to share the journey of life with.

God wants to help you develop your inner circle. Jesus dedicated His life to the twelve, and it was worth all the effort. Your inner circle is just as important. They will mold and shape you while you shape them. Ultimately you'll become more like Jesus in the process. And that's what discipleship is all about.

Chapter Six

Practicing Relational Discipleship in an Organic Circle

Michael Sove picked me up at the Baltimore-Maryland airport, and then we drove two hours to Salisbury. Cary, Michael's wife, was also in the car. As we warmed up, Cary felt the liberty to share her story. "I went through a horrible divorce," she said. "My husband, who professed to be a godly Christian, turned out to be a con artist and drug addict. He preyed on people like me. While we were in Israel, he stole all my money to purchase drugs. And then he left me. He shattered my dream of being a missionary to Israel, and his actions caused intense devastation and shame."

Cary was so hurt and embarrassed by the situation, she wouldn't come out of her house. Her lonely, dark thoughts—spurred on by demons—drove her into an emotional death grip.

Spending time alone didn't help Cary at all. Her individual thoughts, rather than being a comfort, confused and tormented her. Cary needed other people to help untangle her web of confusion.

Someone invited Cary to a small group. She felt warmth and love and was able to share her hurt, struggles, and problems. "They didn't judge me or try to correct me. They just allowed me to share. I realized I wasn't alone in my struggles. I slowly began to understand that perhaps I wasn't abnormal."

But it wasn't human warmth or psychology alone that helped Cary. Yes, her brothers and sisters in the small group used plenty of that. But the small group centered on prayer and the Word of God. God's Word began to speak truth into her life and guided her onto the right path. Larry Crabb says:

> Healing community does not depend on getting people to do what's right or on figuring out what harmful psychological forces are causing us problems and then trying to fix what's wrong. A community that heals is a community that believes the gospel provides forgiveness of all sin, a guaranteed future of perfect community forever, and the freedom now to indulge the deepest desires of our hearts, because the law of God is written within us—we have an appetite for holiness. Communities heal when they focus on releasing what's good.[37]

We live in a nation of individualists. We can do many things alone. But we also need each other. We are part of the body of Christ. We need the Church.

The Greek word for "church" is ekklesia, and it refers to an assembly or gathering. Ekklesia infers that we cannot experience church until we come together—like the writer of Hebrews encourages us to do. I call this chapter "The Organic Circle," because Christ's assembly or church is supernaturally formed by Christ Himself. It's not a man-made circle. It's not a human assembly. Christ, the head of the Church, divinely weaves together His relational body (Ephesians 5:23). As mentioned in the last chapter, we need an inner circle made up of family and friends, but God has also created us to participate in an organic circle, an ekklesia.

Small Enough to Care

In the New Testament, the church location was primarily the home. God used the home environment to mature the early relational disciples. The home was small enough to practice the one-anothers of Scripture and minister to each person.

When Paul wrote about believers serving each other and waiting on each other during the Lord's Supper, he had a small group in mind. When Paul expounds on the operation of spiritual gifts, he envisioned a house-church environment. When he clarifies the role of each member in the body of Christ, he imagined the warm atmosphere of the early house church. John Mallison, small group author, writes, "It is almost certain that every mention of a local church or meeting, whether for worship or fellowship, is in actual fact a reference to a church meeting in a house."[38]

The early church sacrificed their time and physical dwellings to live in community. The Holy Spirit richly blessed those communities, providing an example for the generations to come. Even though they often faced persecution for openly proclaiming the gospel, their God-inspired community shone brightly to their neighbors.

God never intends for a Christian to live as an island. He wants each believer to grow with other fellow Christians. Sadly, many are accustomed to sitting in church, hearing a great message, but they never move beyond the information stage.

The small group, unlike large-group celebration, connects people in face-to-face gatherings. No one can take a back seat; everyone is in the front row. Each member is a priest who ministers.

The intimate environment of the small group helps each person to live the Christian life, not just understand it. The cell or micro church is a place where a person can taste authentic community. It's the place to find a true sense of belonging. People feel more human in small groups. A person has a name, a purpose. There is a group of people who care. Life takes on new meaning.

People use many names for cell groups. At our church we use life groups. Others use touch groups or heart groups. Whatever you call your relational group, it's best to see it as the Church, just as the Sunday worship service is. It simply serves a different purpose. The larger service is to hear teaching and to worship with all those in the local church. The cell is more personal; it's a time to apply God's Word to our daily lives. Putnam and Feldstein say, "In sum, smaller is better for forging and sustaining connections."[39]

What Happens in a Micro Church

Many cell meetings—like ours--include four "Ws:" Welcome, Worship, the Word, and Witness (or Works). All four of these elements help the cell develop community. The icebreaker (Welcome) touches some area of the past, and, though often humorous, it reveals something about the person. Then worship draws the members into the presence of the living God. The cell lesson (the Word) avoids the impersonal, one-man-show mentality and asks each to contribute. Finally, the vision-casting time (witness) requires group involvement—working together to win a lost world to Christ.

While I think the home is the ideal place to meet, it's not the only place. Effective groups meet on university campuses, in parks, in restaurants, or at places of business. I personally love family-oriented small groups, but there are other types of groups as well—men's, women's, youth, and children's groups.

For cells to maintain their ministry focus, they must remain small. Someone once said, "Community begins at three and ends at fifteen." Keeping the group small maintains the community feeling. In the intimacy of a small, closely knit group people will confess their faults one to another in order to be healed (James 5:16). Open sharing becomes difficult when the group grows to more than fifteen. The quest for community should stir each cell to develop new leaders in order to eventually multiply new groups that will offer fresh hope to people in need.

Cells are often the springboard for one-on-one relationships that take place outside the meetings.

Some leaders insist on spending two to three hours in the actual meeting. People leave immediately afterward because of their busy schedules. I strongly recommend that a cell meeting end after one-and-a-half hours to allow time for refreshments and spontaneous interaction. It's often during the refreshment time that the best sharing, evangelism, and community life take place. Not all community or ministry happens in the cell group. Cells are often the springboard for one-on-one relationships that take place outside the meetings.

In my own micro church, we like to break up into smaller groups as well. Usually the men will go to one room and the women in another; if we have children in the group, they will go to another room. In the smaller group, new, additional needs are revealed. Often one of the men will share things that he wouldn't share in the mixed gathering.

Often additional one-on-one meetings take place outside the official cell gathering. Ted needed additional help because he struggled with pornography. John had his own personal struggles. Ted and John agreed to meet at 6 a.m. on Wednesday mornings at Starbucks to share struggles, pray for one another, and to hold each other accountable.

Freedom to Share

As I traveled to Salisbury with Michael and Cary Sove, they shared how God was using the same healing community to transform others. Mike said:

> Jane just came to Christ. Last month she freely shared how her daughter was sexually abused and the internal struggles she experienced. Jane's transparency made all the difference in the atmosphere. People were crying because they could relate to her pain and struggles.

Jane's transparency had a two-fold effect. It opened up others in the group to share their past hurts, but it also brought emotional healing to Jane. She received healing in the process of being intimate and sharing freely about who she was. Then Cary shared a negative example:

> Karen also received Jesus at our church. Yet, she refused to open up to people. She chose to walk by herself. She showed up to Sunday celebration each week but didn't open up her life to others in a

small group atmosphere. We've noticed that those like Karen who only come to the larger gatherings get to know fewer people and don't grow in maturity.

We need to be willing to open our lives and hearts to those around us. The small group is a perfect place to start this process of intimacy. James 5:16 says, "Therefore confess your sins to each other and pray for each other so that you may be healed." All believers are the priests of the living God and the confessional time often happens when we meet together. Crabb says:

> If we see ourselves clearly, we will be able to see into the tangled heart of another (Matthew 7:3-5). But when we do, we must make it our goal to reconnect people with the heart of God through our exposure of their darkness.[40]

How much does someone need to share? Only what he or she is comfortable with. Nothing should be forced or manipulated. Some problems should only be discussed one-on-one.

Learning from the Methodists

John Wesley organized the early Methodists in small groups that they called classes. The class meeting was not a highly organized event. It normally lasted for one hour, and the main event was "reporting on your soul."

The class would begin with an opening song. Then the leader would share a personal, religious experience. Afterwards, he would inquire about the spiritual life of those in the group. Each member would give a testimony about his or her spiritual condition. It was a time of sharing their hearts. Thomas Hawkins writes:

> John Wesley recognized the fundamental connection between discipleship and community. Many other preachers of the English revival engaged in field preaching. Wesley alone organized his followers into small communities that provided a tool kit of practices and a network of companions. Early Methodists discovered that mutual accountability within a spiritual community effectively built up a consistent discipleship.[41]

The methodology of John Wesley followed the advice of John the apostle: "But if we walk in the light, as he is in the light, we have fellowship with one another, and the blood of Jesus, his Son, purifies us from all sin"(1 John 1:7). It's in this light that we have fellowship with one another and that we walk before the living God.

M. Scott Peck reiterates this truth:

> If we are going to use the word [community] meaningfully, we must restrict it to a group of individuals who have learned how to communicate

> honestly with each other, whose
> relationships go deeper than their masks
> of composure, and who have developed
> some significant commitment to
> "rejoice together, mourn together," and
> to "delight in each other, make others'
> conditions our own."[42]

God often channels His healing through others. We should ask Him to help us receive counsel from others. The horizontal plane is enhanced by the vertical one. Jesus infuses grace in each person to minister to others. True Christian community, in fact, only works when Christ's presence and God's Spirit are included in the mix. It's the presence of Jesus within the believer that makes Christian fellowship so delightful. With Jesus' presence among the group , people should expect Him to act so that mutual ministry will occur.

The micro church is specifically designed to tear away the layers of pain and the hidden agendas and to apply God's inerrant Word to real needs. Paul wrote to a micro house church saying, "I myself am convinced, my brothers, that you yourselves are full of goodness, complete in knowledge and competent to instruct one another" (Romans 15:14).

The early house church members had the power within themselves to minister effectively to each other. They weren't powerless, helpless lay people, dependent on an outside source for spiritual growth, such as a teacher, pastor, or apostle. Larry Crabb affirms this truth saying:

> Ordinary people have the power to change other people's lives. . . the power is found in connection, that profound meeting when the truest part of one's soul meets the emptiest recesses in another and finds something there, when life passes from one to the other. When that happens, the giver is left more full than before and the receiver less terrified, eventually eager, to experience even deeper, more mutual connection.[43]

Often our pride erects walls of perfection that hide our gaping needs and separate us from others. I find myself wanting to impress others and keep them at arm's length from my dire needs. The Holy Spirit gently seeks to breakdown my barriers, showing me a much better way. When He does break through, and I open up to others, I not only receive healing but others feel more comfortable in my presence and are more open to share their needs.

Everyone Needs a Family

Recently I walked with pastor Jeff Tunnell in downtown Big Bear, California. Jeff has lived in Big Bear since 1970. He gave me a history lesson as we walked along. "This is where I stood when I first heard the voice of Jesus to give up smoking hash and follow Him," he told me. "That building over there was our church's first meeting place." Then we walked by Chad's bar. "This bar is church for many people in Big Bear. The bartender is the pastor; the liquor is their holy spirit; and the people gather in small groups inside."

Why do people frequent bars? Because they can gather, talk, and not feel judged.

Micro churches have something far better than alcoholic spirits. The God-given Holy Spirit flows within the meeting, opening up hearts and minds. Jesus wants His people to bond as a spiritual family. While centered on the Word of God, the focus is having a place to share together. The order of the meeting is not nearly as important as Christ in the midst and His working through each person. Everyone finds the wholeness they personally long for through giving and receiving. Jesus doesn't want us to hold His life within us. He wants us to give it away. And in the process of giving it away, we experience real life and hope.

John is a good example of this give-and-take process. When he finally decided to attend one of our church's life groups, the hardest part was walking through the door for the first time, but his fears were unfounded. He felt comfortable, and the group didn't pressure him to talk. The next meeting was easier, and he even made a few friends. Within the first month, after hearing others transparently talk about their own needs, he felt comfortable enough to share personal prayer requests. It's been one year now since John joined the cell group. His life has been transformed. His relationship with his wife Mary has also improved. He gets into his car for work each morning knowing he has a cell community with whom he can share his struggles.

He realizes now more than ever that he needs fellow believers as he walks through the Christian life.

Connecting Micro with Macro

Having a smaller spiritual family meets core needs. Yet, smaller groups stay healthier when they are connected in larger networks. Even the secular world acknowledges the strengths of both formats. Robert Putnam and Lewis Feldstein, in *Better Together*, write:

> Create cellular structure with smaller groups linked to form a larger, more encompassing one. Organizational choices that facilitate "mixing" and "bridging" among small groups can harness the benefits of both intimacy and breadth. If training or travels are designed to bring local leaders together, the cellular structure can also help particular success stories spread and so speed institutional learning.[44]

The book of Acts is the history of the formation of the local church. We read that the early believers:

> . . . devoted themselves to the apostles' teaching and to the fellowship, to the breaking of bread and to prayer . . . . Every day they continued to meet together in the temple courts. They broke bread in their homes and ate together with glad and sincere hearts" (Acts 2:42,46).

Paul writes to the Ephesian elders, "You know that I have not hesitated to preach anything that would be helpful to you but have taught you publicly and from house to house" (Acts 20:20). The apostle Paul continued to preach and teach publicly and privately. As long as possible, the Early Church met together openly to hear the apostle's teaching. Yet, they also met from house to house.

The church is God's vessel on earth to save, disciple, and prepare workers to continue the process of reaching people for Christ.

The writers of the New Testament repeatedly referred to the Church as either a group of people in the city or one particular household. When Paul wrote in 1 Corinthians 1:2, "To the church of God in Corinth" he was referring to all believers in the city. Yet at the end of the same book, Paul said, "Aquila and Priscilla greet you warmly in the Lord, and so does the church that meets at their house" (1 Corinthians 16:19). For the first three hundred years after Christ's resurrection, the New Testament Church existed primarily as individual house churches. When possible the house churches in a particular city would celebrate together. Yet, the normal church gathering was in the home.

Whether the Church meets in the home or as a larger community, the true Church consists of those who have placed their faith in Jesus Christ and live under His Lordship. The Church is a spiritual family of brothers and sisters who have the same Father in heaven. The Church is God's vessel on earth to save, disciple, and prepare workers to continue the process of reaching people for Christ.

Accountability

In 1983 when I planted a church in downtown Long Beach, I remember encountering people with an anti-church philosophy. They would argue that the church was unnecessary, since they had a personal relationship with God.

They felt it was sufficient to read their Bibles at home and do church by themselves. I remember trying to argue with them about how God ordained the Church and had raised up an organic body of believers who would come together to encourage one another. My arguments fell flat.

Part of the process of becoming a relational disciple is to submit to God-given authority. Pastors and teachers are God's method of molding relational disciples because they can watch over believers, helping them to become more like Jesus. God-given leaders can help believers find their place in the body of Christ, so that the Church grows and builds itself up in love.

When we first started our church in Moreno Valley, California in 2004, I talked with a family about the need to join one local church. In my first conversation with Vince, the husband, I didn't want to appear legalistic or overbearing but ended up giving him fuzzy, unclear comments. The next morning, however, the Lord spoke to me clearly and reminded me of one of the main reasons why each believer needs to be committed to a local church.

Scripture says in Hebrews 13:17:

> Obey your leaders and submit to their authority. They keep watch over you as men who must give an account. Obey them so that their work will be a joy, not a burden, for that would be of no advantage to you.

God reminded me that He has ordained the local church to "watch over the souls" of believers. The local church is God's plan to care for believers and to help mold them in Christ.

When a person joins the local church, he or she is saying, "I will receive spiritual direction from the local church leadership, and I will also contribute to the local church" (e.g., tithing, using his or her gifts, etc.).

I told Vince that if he and his family made a decision to join our local church, he wasn't making a life-time decision. He could always leave later on. But if and when he did leave, I would then encourage him to once again find another local church.

God has raised up pastors and teachers for the maturing of God's people for greater works of service. These pastors and teachers that God has raised up are there to help mature His body. Ephesians 4: 11-12 says:

> It was he who gave some to be apostles, some to be prophets, some to be evangelists, and some to be pastors and teachers, to prepare God's people for works of service, so that the body of Christ may be built up until we all reach unity in the faith and in the knowledge of the Son of God and become mature, attaining to the whole measure of the fullness of Christ.

We need Christ's Church to grow and develop. God wants us to be accountable to the leaders He has raised up.

I recently visited a neighbor whose sister-in-law had come to our church. She graciously invited us into her house and showed us all the new refurnishing projects she has accomplished. She was obviously very proud of her new house. We asked about her church involvement. She answered by telling us that Christ was in her heart, and that she used to attend an evangelical church in the South, but that she didn't feel the need to attend church anymore. "After all," she said, "you don't have to attend church to be a Christian."

I was impressed by her friendliness but grieved by her view of the Church. I also knew that she would never fully mature into a relational disciple on her own. She desperately needed the body of Christ, but had been vaccinated against it.

So many are just like her, having submitted to Christ but never developed into a relational disciple. Jesus desires to mold us through His Church, the organic body that He has raised up. Jesus doesn't have plan B. Jesus is Lord of His Church and He desires that we become part of it. Yet, it doesn't stop there. Jesus also plans to reach a lost world through His body, the Church.

Chapter Seven

Practicing Relational Discipleship in a Mission Circle

An Intervarsity campus group was consumed with finding ways to attract non-believers. The social events weren't working, in spite of all the invitations and planning. Finally, one of the exasperated workers said, "I'm going to bring my non-Christian friend to the prayer meeting tonight." The campus leader was fearful of what might happen. Would the unbeliever be turned off by the reading of Scripture, Christian worship, and deep sharing?

The unbeliever came to the meeting and enjoyed every moment of it. He was thrilled to see people worshipping. He liked the deep sharing. He tasted authenticity, and it was good!

As they pondered what happened, they came to see that their non-Christian friends were hungry for God, for reality, for relationship. They didn't want the high powered, impersonal programs. They wanted the fire, the warmth, the truth.

The Early Church grew as God lit a fire among the early Christians to live out the Christian life. Acts 2:43-47 says:

> Everyone was filled with awe, and many
> wonders and miraculous signs were done

by the apostles. All the believers were together and had everything in common. Selling their possessions and goods, they gave to anyone as he had need. . . .And the Lord added to their number daily those who were being saved.

When Christ is the acting head of His Church, and His people are in-tune with Him, He adds daily to the Church.

Patrick believed that belonging comes before believing.

When people experience genuine love and servanthood, they sit-up and take notice. Bryan Stone writes:

The most evangelistic thing the Church can do, therefore, is to be the Church not merely in public but as a new and alternative public; not merely in society but as a new and distinct society, a new and unprecedented social existence.[45]

Learning from Saint Patrick

In 2007, I went with my family to Ireland. My last name "Comiskey" is of Irish descent, so we were eager to explore the area. By far the greatest experience of the trip for me was to see where Saint Patrick ministered and to understand the impact

Patrick had on Ireland. I had several very spiritual experiences meditating on Patrick's life and work.

In the Fifth Century AD, when Patrick was about fourteen, he was captured by Irish raiders and taken as a slave to Ireland, where he lived for six years before escaping and returning to his family in England. God saved Patrick, raised him up to become a bishop in the church, and then called him to go back to Ireland as a missionary. Patrick's ministry was so effective that not only was most of Ireland converted, but God used the church in Ireland to send missionaries around the world.

Patrick's model of reaching out to others was highly relational, hospitable, and community-oriented. Patrick and his followers moved into a pagan area, set up shop as a team, and became part of the community. They tried to make the Church accessible. They took seriously the passage in the Book of Psalms that says, "Taste and see that the LORD is good; blessed is the man who takes refuge in him" (34:8). Patrick believed that the truth is first caught and then taught.

Outsiders naturally became part of the Celtic Church. They were invited on a journey of discovery. Patrick and his team reasoned that as people experienced Christian community, they would begin the process of conversion. Patrick believed that belonging comes before believing. He and his fellow missionaries excelled in community outreach, having a place where the seeker could experience God, and eventually participate in the life of the church.

Saint Patrick started a movement, and he did it by developing relationships with the people and engaging their imagination by using symbols they understood (e.g., shamrock to clarify the Trinity). Many have made comparisons with St. Patrick's ministry and our own current situation. Like the civilization in St. Patrick's day, people today are hungry for relationships. They want to taste Christ in their midst and naturally grow in their relationship with Christ.

The Trinity desires the lost to be found and the lonely to have a community.

Churches have spent countless hours trying to figure out how to connect "follow-up" with evangelism. The problem is that step one has been divorced from step two. The relational model offered by Saint Patrick and the early disciples brought people into the community, allowing them to see the change and to become disciples in the process.

Rich Richardson says:

> We need a team to reach our neighborhood. We need a team to reach our workplace. We need a team to reach our postmodern friends. Postmodern people understand the importance of community.[46]

Individuals living in the midst of an informational overload can too easily tuck away the new gospel information in one crevice and do nothing about it. Community must transform them.

The Trinity desires the lost be found and the lonely to have a community. For people to find community they have to see community. Christ's famous prayer for unity among the believers was also a call to reach an unbelieving world. Jesus said:

> My prayer is not for them alone. I pray also for those who will believe in me through their message, that all of them may be one, Father, just as you are in me and I am in you. May they also be in us so that the world may believe that you have sent me. I have given them the glory that you gave me, that they may be one as we are one: I in them and you in me. May they be brought to complete unity to let the world know that you sent me and have loved them even as you have loved me (John 17: 20-23).

As the disciples demonstrated unity among themselves, the world recognized God's supernatural work and believed that He was alive. They recognized that only God could do such an amazing work, and they believed that He existed.

Francis Schaeffer points out:

> People are looking to us to produce something that will bring the world to a standstill—human beings treating human beings like human beings. The church should be able to do this because we know who we are and we know who they are—first, men made in the image of God, then brothers within the church and Christian community on the basis of the shed blood of the Lord Jesus. Christ.[47]

Evangelism as a Group Event

As a teenager, I used to fish each year in Ensenada, Mexico. My family camped at Estero Beach, and I found my favorite spot on a rock near the entrance. I remember casting out my reel with two hooks and bringing in two decent size bass. Then we cooked the fish, sat around the campfire, and ate a delicious meal. I will never forget those days.

One thing I've never done is fish with nets. I've only fished for pleasure and net fishing seems like a serious undertaking.

The disciples of Jesus were serious fisherman. They fished for a living and net fishing was the tool of the trade. Mark says:

> As Jesus walked beside the Sea of Galilee, he saw Simon and his brother Andrew casting a net into the lake, for they were fishermen. "Come, follow me," Jesus said, "and I will make you fishers of men." At once they left their nets and followed him. When he had gone a little farther, he saw James, son of Zebedee, and his brother John in a boat, preparing their nets (Mark 1:16-20).

When the disciples cast out their nets, they did it as a group. When Jesus told them that He would make them fishers of men, He was also thinking about group fishing. Jesus never sent the disciples out alone. He wanted His disciples to live out the Gospel before others so that the unbelievers might see their changed lives and believe in Him.

Group evangelism takes the pressure off one person. The group works better together. Paul says in 1 Corinthians 14: 23ff:

> So if the whole church comes together and everyone speaks in tongues, and some who do not understand or some unbelievers come in, will they not say that you are out of your mind? But if an unbeliever or someone who does not understand comes in while everybody is prophesying, he will be convinced by all that he is a sinner and will be judged by all, and the secrets of his heart will be laid bare. So he will fall down and

worship God, exclaiming, "God is really among you!"

When the Scripture says "everyone was prophesying," it literally means that everyone participated. Paul is talking to a house church, in which everyone was involved. The word "prophesy" in this passage refers to each person ministering or speaking into the life of the unbeliever that enters the house.

When the unbeliever entered the room of Christ followers, prophesy began to flow naturally as the individual believers longed to minister to the needs of the unbelieving visitor.

And so it is today. Cell groups come to life when an unbeliever attends. The members exercise their gifts in a new, fresh way.

Transparent Sharing

Evangelism in a small group involves natural sharing. Non-Christians can ask questions, share doubts, and talk about their own spiritual journey. Sharing openly gives unbelievers a new sense of hope as they realize that Christians have weaknesses and struggles too. More than an explanation, the "gospel" in the small group is seen and felt. I like the advice of Richard Peace, professor at Fuller Theological Seminary. He says in his book, *Small Group Evangelism*:

> In a successful small group, love, acceptance, and fellowship flow in

unusual measure. This is the ideal situation in which to hear about the kingdom of God. In this context, the "facts of the gospel" come through not as cold proposition but as living truths visible in the lives of others. In such an atmosphere, a person is irresistibly drawn to Christ by his gracious presence.[48]

As each member reveals how Christ has worked in their lives, unbelievers are attracted to Jesus. The more we can expose the unbeliever to Christ in us, the better. A person will enter into community where love and acceptance is the norm. Rich Richardson says:

Today people are looking for a community to belong to before a message to believe in. Evangelism is about helping people belong so that they come to believe. Most people today do not "decide" to believe. In community they "discover" that they believe, and then they decide to affirm that publicly and to follow Christ intentionally. People are looking for a safe, accepting place to develop their identity and sense of self in community.[49]

Transparent sharing, love, and acceptance reveal to non-Christians that believers are not perfect—just forgiven. One of Satan's chief tactics is legalistic deception, trying to convince people that God requires unreachable standards and that only "good" people enter heaven. Small-group evangelism can correct this misconception.

Developing Relationships

For group evangelism to work effectively, it means that each group member will develop personal relationships with unbelievers.

Jesus demonstrated the importance of relationships. Not only did He develop a deep, lasting relationship with twelve disciples, but He also was constantly reaching out to those around Him. He spoke with the woman at the well in Samaria and with great grace pointed out her true need. Jesus allowed Himself to be diverted if someone needed help.

The Early Church followed Christ's example by imitating Him as they lived with those around them. The first place of witness for the Early Church was the household. The Greek word for household is *oikos*. Back in those days a household, or *oikos*, included more than the family. *Oikos* relationships embraced family members, slaves, friends, and working acquaintances.

Oikos relationships today comprise family, friends, work associates, or anyone you spend one hour or more per week with.

If your *oikos* network is lacking, there are ways to expand it. Often, relationships with non-Christians are developed in the context of something else. For example, if you get involved in the normal social scene, you earn the right to share names with one another. Coaching softball, going to one particular hairdresser, joining the volunteer board at the home association, or getting involved in a special interest group are among the many ways to build relationships. Developing business colleagues, sport associates, and special interests and hobby associates are other ways to broaden your friendship base.

Communities are eager for volunteers to serve in social action programs, whether it is daycare, counseling, outreach to the homeless, or some other program. In every community there is an opportunity to share love and Christian values in a positive way. You can join a parent/teacher association, neighborhood watch, or one of the many other committees and organizations that make up our local communities

We've been getting to know our neighbors since returning from Ecuador in 2001. We invited them over for meals, asked if they had particular prayer requests, and brought them baked good during the holidays. We developed a relationship with them.

When we invited our next door neighbors to join our home group, the husband said, "We can't make it on Tuesday night, but our youngest daughter would like you to baptize her." I said, "I'd be thrilled to do that. However, I'd like to take her and you through an equipping process in preparation for baptism." I began to take the entire family through our church's equipping process (see appendix).

The first lesson was about knowing God, and each of them prayed the sinner's prayer as part of the lesson. We then continued to go through the book, in a relaxed, relational setting in their own home. I had the privilege of baptizing their daughter, and we continue to go through the entire equipping process together.

Making friends doesn't have to be a difficult task. It can be part of our natural routine, as we go about our lives. The relational disciple always asks the Holy Spirit to open doors to develop relationships. He in turn opens the way to share the Good News about Jesus.

God is Transforming Us

God uses people to mold and shape us. The imprisoned Paul calls his "dearly beloved son in the faith," Timothy, to come to him in prison in the last days of his life. He longed for Timothy to be near. Paul had not forgotten the tears Timothy shed when they last parted (2 Timothy 1:4). Remembering the congregation in Thessalonica, Paul prays "night and day" to see their faces (1 Thessalonians 3:10).

The aged John knows that his joy will not be full until he can come to his own people and speak face-to-face instead of just writing to them (2 John 12).

When we live in isolation, we can easily lose proper perspective on life. There is no objective voice calling us toward balance. Our point of view becomes clouded, and things tend to seem worse (or better) than they really are.

God is in the process of transforming us to be relational disciples. The world wants to conform us to the pattern of individualism, but God desires to transform us into His very nature. And just as He lives in perfect harmony, He calls us to do the same.

The Good News is that the Trinity lives within us and is powerful to mold us into relational disciples.

Let us resist conforming to today's culture of robust individualism. Let us ask God to make us relational disciples who fulfill the one-anothers of Scripture. As we develop deep, intimate relationships with those who know us best, we can then spread out to others and ultimately reach a lost world for Jesus Christ.

Training for Relational Disciples

To prepare relational disciples, I recommend having a process that moves a person from point A to B. My book, *Leadership Explosion*, describes different equipping tracks that churches use.

I've developed my own equipping track that takes a person from conversion all the way to facilitating a small group, or being part of a team. Each book in my equipping series contains eight lessons. Each lesson has interactive activities that helps the trainee reflect on the lesson in a personal, practical way.

The person being trained should also participate in a small group in order to experience community while learning about it.

I begin with a book on basic biblical truths called *Live*. This book covers key Christian doctrines, including baptism and the Lord's Supper.

The next book is *Encounter*, which guides the believer to receive freedom from sinful bondages. The *Encounter* book can be used one-on-one or in a group.

Then the trainee uses *Grow*, to learn the spiritual practice of daily devotional time. *Grow* gives step-by-step instruction for having a daily quiet time, so that the believer will be able to feed himself or herself through spending daily time with God.

Then the person studies *Share*, which helps him or her learn how to evangelize. This book instructs the believer how to communicate the gospel message in an appealing, personal way. This book also has two lessonss on small group evangelism.

The fifth book is called *Lead*. This book prepares the person to launch a cell, or be part of a leadership team.

The trainee is exercising his or her spiritual muscles in the cell group while completing the five books. I have two other books (*Coach* and *Discover*) that are part of my advanced level training. The book *Discover* focuses on how a cell leader can discover his or her own spiritual gifts (s) and help others in the group find theirs. My book *Coach* helps a small group leader coach someone else who is leading a group.

Some people believe that the only way to train new believers is one-on-one. Others disagree and train new believers in a group setting. Don't confuse the training methodology (where and how you train people) with the training track itself.

There are a great variety of methodologies for implementing discipleship training (e.g., one-on-one discipleship, training after the cell group meeting, training during Sunday school hour, seminars, retreats, or a combination of them all). Many teach the training track during the Sunday school hour, which is often connected to the worship service. I do suggest, however, that those who can't attend during that time slot be given the freedom to take the same training before the cell starts, after the cell finishes, during a day-long training in a home, or be given other options to complete the training.

The training material mentioned here can be purchased from *Joel Comiskey Group* by calling toll-free 1-888-344-CELL (2355) or by ordering at: www.joelcomiskeygroup.com

Resources by Joel Comiskey

Joel Comiskey's previous books cover the following topics

- Leading a cell group (*How to Lead a Great Cell Group Meeting, 2001, 2009*).
- How to multiply the cell group (*Home Cell Group Explosion, 1998*).
- How to prepare spiritually for cell ministry (*An Appointment with the King, 2002*).
- How to practically organize your cell system (*Reap the Harvest,1999; Cell Church Explosion, 2004*).
- How to train future cell leaders (*Leadership Explosion, 2001; Live, 2007; Encounter, 2007; Grow, 2007; Share, 2007; Lead, 2007; Coach, 2008; Discover, 2008*).
- How to coach/care for cell leaders (*How to be a Great Cell Group Coach, 2003; Groups of Twelve, 2000; From Twelve to Three, 2002*).
- How the gifts of the Spirit work within the cell group (*The Spirit-filled Small Group, 2005, 2009; Discover, 2008*).
- How to fine tune your cell system (*Making Cell Groups Work Navigation Guide, 2003*).
- Principles from the second largest church in the world (*Passion and Persistence, 2004*).
- How cell church works in North America (*The Church that Multiplies, 2007, 2009*).
- How to plant a church (*Planting Churches that Reproduce, 2009*)

All of the books listed are available from *Joel Comiskey Group* **by calling toll-free 1-888-344-CELL (2355) or by ordering at:**
www.joelcomiskeygroup.com

How To Lead A Great Cell Group Meeting: So People Want to Come Back

Do people expectantly return to your group meetings every week? Do you have fun and experience joy during your meetings? Is everyone participating in discussion and ministry? You can lead a great cell group meeting, one that is life changing and dynamic. Most people don't realize that they can create a God-filled atmosphere because they don't know how. Now the secret is out. This guide will show you how to:

- Prepare yourself spiritually to hear God during the meeting
- Structure the meeting so it flows
- Spur people in the group to participate and share their lives openly
- Share your life with others in the group
- Create stimulating questions
- Listen effectively to discover what is transpiring in others' lives
- Encourage and edify group members
- Open the group to non-Christians
- See the details that create a warm atmosphere

By implementing these time-tested ideas, your group meetings will become the hot-item of your members' week. They will go home wanting more and return each week bringing new people with them. 140 pgs.

Home Cell Group Explosion: How Your Small Group Can Grow and Multiply

The book crystallizes the author's findings in some eighteen areas of research, based on a meticulous questionnaire that he submitted to cell church leaders in eight countries around the world, locations that he also visited personally for his research. The detailed notes in the back of the book offer the student of cell church growth a rich mine for further reading. The beauty of Comiskey's book is that he not only summarizes his survey results in a thoroughly convincing way but goes on to analyze in practical ways many of his survey results in separate chapters. The happy result is that any cell church leader, intern or member completing this quick read will have his priorities/values clearly aligned and ready to be followed-up. If you are a pastor or small group leader, you should devour this book! It will encourage you and give you simple, practical steps for dynamic small group life and growth. 175 pgs.

An Appointment with the King: *Ideas for Jump-Starting Your Devotional Life*

With full calendars and long lists of things to do, people often put on hold life's most important goal: building an intimate relationship with God. Often, believers wish to pursue the goal but are not sure how to do it. They feel frustrated or guilty when their attempts at personal devotions seem empty and unfruitful. With warm, encouraging writing, Joel Comiskey guides readers on how to set a daily appointment with the King and make it an exciting time they will look forward to. This book first answers the question "Where do I start?" with step-by-step instructions on how to spend time with God and practical ideas for experiencing him more fully. Second, it highlights the benefits of spending time with God, including joy, victory over sin, and spiritual guidance. The book will help Christians tap into God's resources on a daily basis, so that even in the midst of busyness they can walk with him in intimacy and abundance. 175 pgs.

Reap the Harvest: *How a Small Group System Can Grow Your Church*

Have you tried small groups and hit a brick wall? Have you wondered why your groups are not producing the fruit that was promised? Are you looking to make your small groups more effective? Cell-church specialist and pastor Dr. Joel Comiskey studied the world's most successful cell churches to determine why they grow. The key: They have embraced specific principles. Conversely, churches that do not embrace these same principles have problems with their groups and therefore do not grow. Cell churches are successful not because they have small groups but because they can support the groups. In this book, you will discover how these systems work. 236 pgs.

La Explosión de la Iglesia Celular: *Cómo Estructurar la Iglesia en Células Eficaces* (Editorial Clie, 2004)

This book is only available in Spanish and contains Joel Comiskey's research of eight of the world's largest cell churches, five of which reside in Latin America. It details how to make the transition from a traditional church to the cell church structure and many other valuable insights, including: the history of the cell church, how to organize your church to become a praying church, the most important principles of the cell church, and how to raise up an army of cell leaders. 236 pgs.

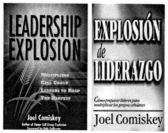

Leadership Explosion: *Multiplying Cell Group Leaders to Reap the Harvest*

Some have said that cell groups are leader breeders. Yet even the best cell groups often have a leadership shortage. This shortage impedes growth and much of the harvest goes untouched. Joel Comiskey has discovered why some churches are better at raising up new cell leaders than others. These churches do more than pray and hope for new leaders. They have an intentional strategy, a plan that will quickly equip as many new leaders as possible. In this book, you will discover the training models these churches use to multiply leaders. You will discover the underlying principles of these models so that you can apply them.
202 pgs.

FIVE-BOOK EQUIPPING SERIES

#1: Live   #2: Encounter   #3: Grow   #4: Share   #5: Lead

The five book equipping series is designed to train a new believer all the way to leading his or her own cell group. Each of the five books contains eight lessons. Each lesson has interactive activities that helps the trainee reflect on the lesson in a personal, practical way.

Live starts the training by covering key Christian doctrines, including baptism and the Lord's supper. 85 pgs.

Encounter guides the believer to receive freedom from sinful bondages. The Encounter book can be used one-on-one or in a group. 91 pgs.

Grow gives step-by-step instruction for having a daily quiet time, so that the believer will be able to feed him or herself through spending daily time with God. 87 pgs.

Share instructs the believer how to communicate the gospel message in a winsome, personal way. This book also has two chapters on small group evangelism. 91 pgs.

Lead prepares the Christian on how to facilitate an effective cell group. This book would be great for those who form part of a small group team. 91 pgs.

TWO-BOOK ADVANCED TRAINING SERIES

COACH   DISCOVER

Coach and Discover make-up the Advanced Training, prepared specifically to take a believer to the next level of maturity in Christ.

Coach prepares a believer to coach another cell leader. Those experienced in cell ministry often lack understanding on how to coach someone else. This book provides step-by-step instruction on how to coach a new cell leader from the first meeting all the way to giving birth to a new group. The book is divided into eight lessons, which are interactive and help the potential coach deal with real-life, practical coaching issues. 85 pgs.

Discover clarifies the twenty gifts of the Spirit mentioned in the New Testament. The second part shows the believer how to find and use his or her particular gift. This book is excellent to equip cell leaders to discover the giftedness of each member in the group. 91 pgs.

How to be a Great Cell Group Coach: Practical insight for Supporting and Mentoring Cell Group Leaders

Research has proven that the greatest contributor to cell group success is the quality of coaching provided for cell group leaders. Many are serving in the position of a coach, but they don't fully understand what they are supposed to do in this position. Joel Comiskey has identified seven habits of great cell group coaches. These include: Receiving from God, Listening to the needs of the cell group leader, Encouraging the cell group leader, Caring for the multiple aspects of a leader's life, Developing the cell leader in various aspects of leadership, Strategizing with the cell leader to create a plan, Challenging the cell leader to grow.

Practical insights on how to develop these seven habits are outlined in section one. Section two addresses how to polish your skills as a coach with instructions on diagnosing problems in a cell group, how to lead coaching meetings, and what to do when visiting a cell group meeting. This book will prepare you to be a great cell group coach, one who mentors, supports, and guides cell group leaders into great ministry. 139 pgs.

Groups of Twelve: *A New Way to Mobilize Leaders and Multiply Groups in Your Church*

This book clears the confusion about the Groups of 12 model. Joel dug deeply into the International Charismatic Mission in Bogota, Colombia and other G12 churches to learn the simple principles that G12 has to offer your church. This book also contrasts the G12 model with the classic 5x5 and shows you what to do with this new model of ministry. Through onsite research, international case studies, and practical experience, Joel Comiskey outlines the G12 principles that your church can use today.

Billy Hornsby, director of the Association of Related Churches, says, "Joel Comiskey shares insights as a leader who has himself raised up numerous leaders. From how to recognize potential leaders to cell leader training to time-tested principles of leadership--this book has it all. The accurate comparisons of various training models make it a great resource for those who desire more leaders. Great book!" 182 pgs.

From Twelve To Three: *How to Apply G12 Principles in Your Church*

The concept of the Groups of 12 began in Bogota, Colombia, but now it is sweeping the globe. Joel Comiskey has spent years researching the G12 structure and the principles behind it.

From his experience as a pastor, trainer, and consultant, he has discovered that there are two ways to embrace the G12 concept: adopting the entire model or applying the principles that support the model.

This book focuses on the application of principles rather than adoption of the entire model. It outlines the principles and provides a modified application which Joel calls the G12.3. This approach presents a pattern that is adaptable to many different church contexts.

The concluding section illustrates how to implement the G12.3 in various kinds of churches, including church plants, small churches, large churches, and churches that already have cells. 178 pgs.

The Spirit-filled Small Group: *Leading Your Group to Experience the Spiritual Gifts.*
The focus in many of today's small groups has shifted from Spirit-led transformation to just another teacher-student Bible study. But exercising every member's spiritual gifts is vital to the effectiveness of the group. With insight born of experience in more than twenty years of small group ministry, Joel Comiskey explains how leaders and participants alike can be supernaturally equipped to deal with real-life issues. Put these principles into practice and your small group will never be the same!

This book works well with Comiskey's training book, ***Discover.*** It fleshes out many of the principles in Comiskey's training book. Chuck Crismier, radio host, Viewpoint, writes, "Joel Comiskey has again provided the Body of Christ with an important tool to see God's Kingdom revealed in and through small groups." 191 pgs.

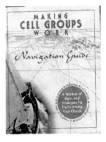

Making Cell Groups Work Navigation Guide: *A Toolbox of Ideas and Strategies for Transforming Your Church.*
For the first time, experts in cell group ministry have come together to provide you with a 600 page reference tool like no other. When Ralph Neighbour, Bill Beckham, Joel Comiskey and Randall Neighbour compiled new articles and information under careful orchestration and in-depth understanding that Scott Boren brings to the table, it's as powerful as private consulting! Joel Comiskey has an entire book within this mammoth 600 page work. There are also four additional authors.

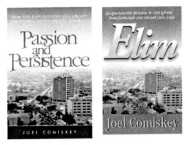

Passion and Persistence: *How the Elim Church's Cell Groups Penetrated an Entire City for Jesus*
This book describes how the Elim Church in San Salvador grew from a small group to 116,000 people in 10,000 cell groups. Comiskey takes the principles from Elim and applies them to churches in North America and all over the world.

Ralph Neighbour says: "I believe this book will be remember as one of the most important ever written about a cell church movement! I experienced the *passion* when visiting Elim many years ago. Comiskey's report about Elim is not a *pattern* to be slavishly copied. It is a journey into grasping the true theology and methodology of the New Testament church. You'll discover how the Elim Church fans into flame their passion for Jesus and His Word, how they organize their cells to penetrate a city and world for Jesus, and how they persist until God brings the fruit." 158 pgs.

The Church that Multiplies: *Growing a Healthy Cell Church in North America.*

Does the cell church strategy work in North America? We hear about exciting cell churches in Colombia and Korea, but where are the dynamic North American cell churches? This book not only declares that the cell church concept does work in North America but dedicates an entire chapter to examining North American churches that are successfully using the cell strategy to grow in quality and quantity. This book provides the latest statistical research about the North American church and explains why the cell church approach restores health and growth to the church today. More than anything else, this book will provide practical solutions for pastors and lay leaders to use in implementing cell-based ministry. 181 pgs.

Planting Churches that Reproduce: *Planting a Network of Simple Churchces.*

What is the best way to plant churches in the 21st century? Comiskey believes that simple, reproducible church planting is most effective. The key is to plant churches that are simple enough to grow into a movement of churches. Comiskey has been gathering material for this book for the past fifteen Years. He has also planted three churches in a wide variety of settings. Planting Churches that Reproduce is the fruit of his research and personal experience. Comiskey uses the latest North American church planting statistics, but extends the illustrations to include worldwide church planting. More than anything else, this book will provide practical solutions for those planting churches today. Comiskey's book is a must-read book for all those interested in establishing Christ-honoring, multiplying churches. 176 pgs.

Index

A

Alexis de Tocqueville   22
Americans   23, 24, 25, 26, 27,
  32, 65, 151
Anne   9, 82, 83, 87, 151
Anne White   9
Anonymity   11, 5
Athanasian Creed   37
Augustine   38

B

baptism   146
Bernard Madoff   69
Biblical culture   16
Big Bear   117, 118
Billy Graham   53
bitterness   49, 50, 63, 71, 72,
  81, 82, 83, 84, 86, 88,
  102
Bowling   26, 27, 157
Brian McLemore   9
Buddy Lindsay   28

C

C.S. Lewis   72
California   3, 28, 68, 82, 117,
  121, 157
Calvary Chapel   136
Care-fronting   79
Cary Sove   107, 113
celebration   78, 110, 113
cell   2, 143, 143, 144, 143,
  143, 145, 145, 145, 144,
  146, 147, 148, 149, 150
Cell Church   78, 143, 150
Cell churches   145
Cell Church Solutions   78
Cell leader, leadership
Celtic Church   127
Challenging   147
character deficiencies   76
Christianity Today   31, 157, 158
church leadership   73, 122
class meeting   114
Coach   140, 143, 147, 152
Coaching   139

Comiskey   1, 53, 94, 126, 143,
     2, 3, 144, 145, 147, 148,
     152, 153, 4, 146, 149,
     150, 7
community   2, 3, 4, 16, 25, 28,
     30, 31, 33, 35, 36, 37,
     40, 41, 42, 43, 46, 74,
     75, 85, 93, 94, 102, 108,
     85, 108, 110, 111, 112,
     113, 115, 116, 119, 120,
     127, 128, 129, 130, 133,
     135, 139
Confession   59
Conflict   6, 75, 76, 96

D

Dan Blazer   52
David Augsberger   79
David Olson   12
David Shi   65
Depression   52, 158
Devotional   145
Dietrich Bonhoeffer   42, 158
disciple-making   4, 96
disciples   3, 4, 13, 14, 16, 21,
     32, 39, 40, 41, 47, 48,
     49, 52, 62, 69, 72, 74,
     76, 79, 88, 92, 94, 99,
     103, 109, 121, 128, 129,
     130, 131, 134, 137, 139

discipleship   12, 13, 14, 56,
     100, 105, 115, 56, 140,
     137, 100, 105, 115, 137,
     140, 12, 13, 14
Discover   140, 143, 147, 149
Dylan   21

E

Early Church   14, 16, 63, 66,
     120, 125, 134
Ecuador   14, 15, 27, 80, 135,
     14, 15, 27, 80, 135, 152
ekklesia   108, 109
Elim Church   149, 149
emerging church   33
Encounter   139, 143, 139, 143,
     146, 146, 152
Encouraging   147
evangelism   3, 13, 112, 128,
     131, 134, 140, 146, 146,
     152
Evangelism Explosion   82

F

Family   6, 98, 117, 7
fellowship   59, 62, 64, 78, 84,
     109, 115, 116, 119, 132
forgive   50, 61, 76, 82, 83, 84,
     85, 86, 87, 88
Forgiveness   86, 87, 88

four Ws: 111

Francis Schaeffer 130, 159

Friendship 103, 104

friendships 27, 102, 103, 104

G

Gareth Hogg 10

Generation Next 33, 152

Gifts 67, 152, 149

Gifts of the Spirit

Glenn Spark 27

gossip 39, 51, 63, 76

grace 12, 17, 50, 58, 59, 60,
61, 67, 68, 76, 81, 83,
95, 96, 97, 116, 134

Greek 21, 22, 51, 66, 84, 108,
134

Group Evangelism 125

group evangelism 134, 140,
146

Groups of Twelve 143, 148

Grow 139, 143, 144, 145, 146

H

healing 71, 77, 84, 86, 113,
116, 117

Healing community 108

Hitler 64

Hope Alliance 82

Hospitality 6, 68

house church 56, 66, 109, 116,
132

humility 39, 43, 60, 74

I

Increased mobility 27

Individual achievement 25

individualism 3, 11, 14, 16, 22,
23, 24, 25, 42, 137, 4, 5

individualist 35

individualistic culture 14

inerrant Word 16, 116, 16,
116, 152

inner circles 96, 98

Isolationism 24, 25

J

James Street 32

Jay 9, 72, 152

Jay Stanwood 9

Jeff Tunnell 117

Jim Carey 48

Joel Comiskey Group 2

joelcomiskeygroup.com 1, 2

John and Mary Reith 10

John Mallison 109, 158

John Maxwell 93

John Wesley 114, 115

Joseph 81, 82

Jżrgen Moltmann 40

K

Kevin Strong   104
Kindness   53, 54
Kirk Hadaway   31, 157

L

Larry Crabb   36, 61, 85, 108,
    116, 158
Lead   140
Leadership   143
leadership   146, 147, 148
Leadership Explosion   139, 143,
    146
Lewis Feldstein   119, 158
Listening   147, 147
Live   6, 62, 63, 139, 143, 146
local church   93, 109, 110, 119,
    121, 122
loneliness   16, 24, 82
lonely people   24, 26
Lone Ranger   22
long-term relationships   27

M

Malachi   101, 102
Mark Galli   31, 91, 157
marriage   83, 95, 96, 97, 101,
    103
Mary Franciscus   44
Media Isolation   5, 29

Methodists   7, 114, 115
Michael Ferris   100
micro church   93, 110, 112, 116
Mike Mason   50, 54, 57, 77,
    158
Moreno Valley   2, 68, 121, 153

N

New Testament   14, 33, 39, 41,
    67, 68, 109, 120, 147,
    149, 153
New Testament church   149
North America   149
North American Church   12

O

oikodomeo   51
oikos   134
Oliver Lutz   10
organic body   67, 121, 123
Organic Circle   7, 107, 109

P

para-church ministry   91
parents   26, 28, 93, 96, 98, 99,
    100, 102, 157
Penetration   126
Persistence   143, 149
Pharaoh   81

Philip Kenneson   32
Phyllis Comiskey   53
Plato   100
Ponzi scheme   69
pornography   113
post-modern culture   33
Postmodern   128
Promise Keeper   93

R

Ralph Neighbour   149
Refrigerator Rights   27, 103
relational body   109
relational disciple   2, 16, 17, 35,
   87, 98, 121, 123, 136, 137, 4
Relational Discipleship   5, 33, 89,
   91, 107, 125, 6, 7
relationships   4, 12, 14, 26, 27,
   28, 33, 36, 41, 57, 63, 93,
   100, 101, 102, 112, 116,
   128, 134, 135, 136, 137
Resources by Joel Comiskey   143
Richard Peace   132, 159
Rich Richardson   128, 133, 159
Rob Campbell   9
Robert Putman   26
Robert Putnam   30, 119, 158
Romans   22, 36, 51, 55, 56, 61,
   64, 66, 73, 116

S

Saint Patrick   7, 126, 128
Salisbury   107, 113
Scott Boren   2, 10, 149
Scott Peck   24, 115, 153, 157
Share   7, 113, 140, 143, 144, 146
sinful nature   59, 69, 70, 72
smaller group   112
small groups   145, 149
social activities   28
social relationship   26, 40
South America   27
Spirit of God   31, 42
spiritual gifts   51, 109, 140, 149
Spiritual Growth   6, 99
Starbucks   113
Steve Cordle   9
Susan Osborn   2, 10

T

Television   29
Thomas Hawkins   115, 158
transformation   31, 42, 149
transparency   3, 104, 113
transparent   58, 105
Transparent sharing   133
Trinity   5, 35, 37, 38, 39, 40, 41,
   42, 46, 60, 128, 5, 41
Triune God   16, 35, 129, 137
TV   11, 26, 29, 30, 91, 157

U

unforgiveness   84, 86, 88

V

vulnerable   58

W

Will Miller   27

Endnotes

1. Robert N. Bellah, et al., Habits of the Heart (Berkley: University of California Press, 1996), p. 37.
2. Ibid.
3. George Gallup Jr., The People's Religion (New York: MacMillan, 1989), as quoted in Andy Stanley and Bill Willits, Creating Community (Sister, Oregon: Multnomah Publishers, 2004), p. 22.
4. M. Scott Peck, The Different Drummer (New York: Simon & Schuster, 1987), p. 58.
5. George Barna as quoted in Julie Gorman, Community That Is Christian (Wheaton: Victor Books, 1993), p. 81.
6. John L. Locke, The De-Voicing of Society (New York: Simon & Schuster, 1998), p. 132.
7. Robert D. Putman, Bowling Alone (New York: Simon & Schuster, 2000), p. 223.
8. Putnam believes that 50% of the social decline is generational. Yet, the other 50% of isolationism comes from excessive media focus (25%), flight to the suburbs (10%), and driving alone to work (15%). Ibid.,p. 284.
9. Ibid., p. 204.
10. Ibid., p. 222.
11. Ibid., p. 245.
12. Jeanne Sather, "TV: How Many Hours Will Your Kids Watch Today?" Accessed at Sunday, June 23, 2002 at http://encarta.msn.com/parents/features/toomuchTV.asp.
13. Ibid., p. 224.
14. C. Kirk Hadaway, Francis M. DuBose, and Stuart A. Wright, Home Cell Groups and House Churches (Nashville: Broadman Press, 1987), p. 211.
15. Mark Galli, "Is the Gay Marriage Debate Over?" Christianity Today (July 2009), p. 33.
16. Philip D. Kenneson and James L. Street, Selling Out the Church: The Dangers of Church Marketing (Nashville: Abingdon Press, 1997), p. 15.
17. Ibid., p. 16.

18. As quoted in Randy Frazee, The Connecting Church (Grand Rapids: Zondervan, 2001), p. 13.

19. E. Moltmann-Wendel and J. Moltmann, Humanity in God (New York: Pilgrim, 1983), p. 97, as quoted in Gorman, op. cit., p. 26.

20. An Appointment with the King (Grand Rapids: Chosen Books, 2002). Can be purchased on my online bookstore at: http://store.joelcomiskeygroup.com/allbobyjoco.html

21. Dietrich Bonhoeffer, Life Together (New York: Harper & Row, 1954), . 20.

22. Mike Mason, The Practice of the Presence of People (Colorado Springs: Waterbrook Press, 1999), pp. 187-188.

23. Dan G. Blazer, "The Depression Epidemic," Christianity Today (March 2009), p. 27.

24. Mason, op. cit., pp. 192.

25. Ibid., pp. 162-63.

26. Bonhoeffer, op. cit., p. 111.

27. Ibid., p. 118.

28. Larry Crabb, Connecting (Nashville: Word Publishing, 1997), p. 47.

29. Mason, op. cit., p. 154.

30. Edward Stewart, American Cultural Patterns: A Cross-Cultural Perspective (Chicago: Intercultural Press, Inc., 1972), p. 36.

31. Mason, op. cit., p. 154.

32. David Augsburger, Caring Enough to Confront (Ventura: Regal Books, 1981), pp. 9-10.

33. Crabb, op. cit., p. 46.

34. Galli, op. cit., p. 33.

35. Mason, op. cit., p. 106.

36. Michael Farris, What a Daughter Needs from Her Dad (Minneapolis: Bethany House, 2004), p. 26.

37. Crabb, op.cit., p. 38.

38. John Mallison, Growing Christians in Small Groups (London: Scripture Union, 1989), p. 5.

39. Robert Putnam and Lewis Feldstein, Better Together (New York: Simon & Schuster, 2003), p. 277.

40. Crabb, op. cit., p. 20.

41. Thomas Hawkins, Cultivating Christian Community (Nashville: Discipleship Resources, 2001), p. 29.

42. Peck, op. cit., p. 59.

43. Crabb, op. cit., p. 31.

44. Putnam and Feldstein, op. cit., p. 279.

45. Bryan Stone, Evangelism after Christendom, (Grand Rapids: Brazos Press, 2007), p. 16.

46. Rich Richardson, Evangelism Outside the Box (Downers Grove: InterVarsity Press, 2000), p. 65.
47. Francis Schaeffer, The Church at the End of the Twentieth Century (Wheaton: Crossway Books, 1994), p. 71.
48. Richard Peace, Small Group Evangelism (Pasadena: Fuller Press, 1996), p.36.
49. Richardson, Ibid., p. 100.